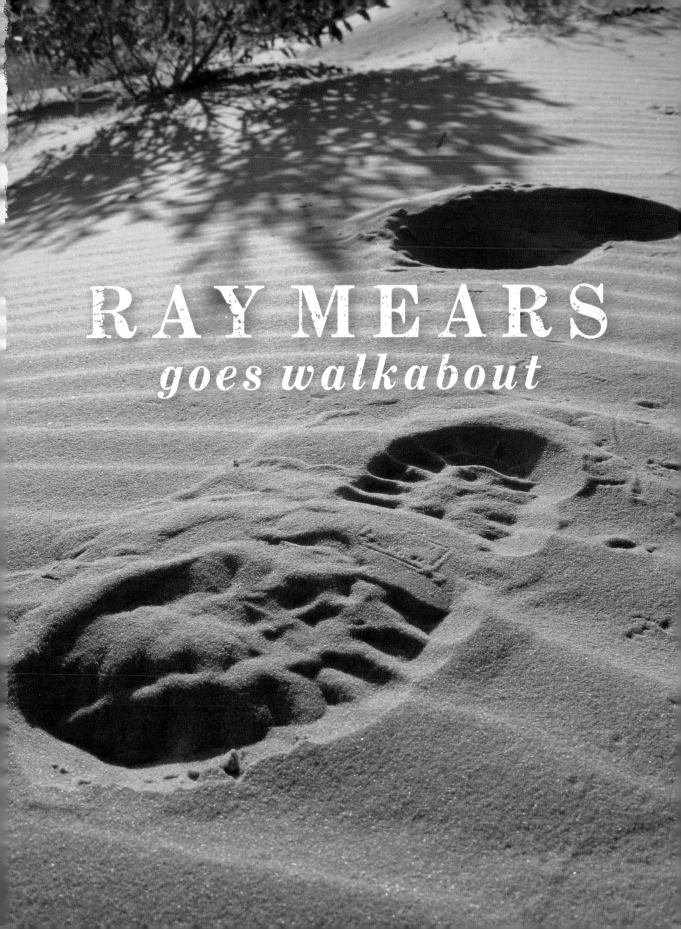

RAY MEARS
goes walkabout

RAY MEARS

goes walkabout

HODDER &
STOUGHTON

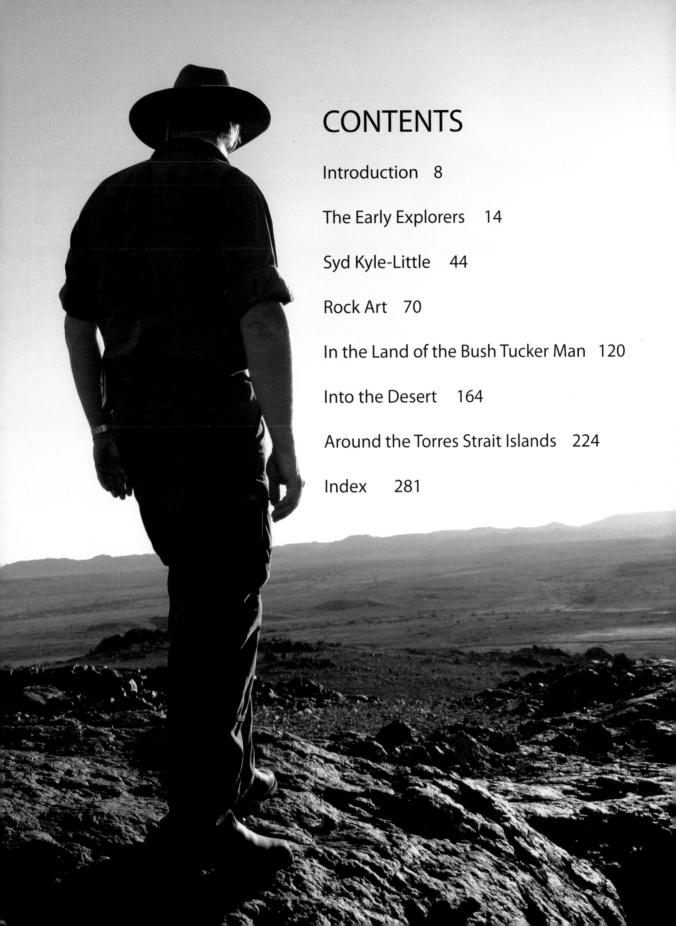

CONTENTS

Rock
Art

DARWIN

Arnhem
Land

ROCK ART

KIMBERLEY

PLATEAU

NORTHERN
TERRITORY
Sturt
Plain

LAGRANGE
BAY

Great Sandy
Desert

Tanami
Desert

Airstrip

GIBSON
Desert

Great
Victoria
DESERT

WESTERN

AUSTRALIA

SOUTH

AUSTRALIA

Perth

Roper
River
camp
TORRES
STRAIT

GULF
OF
CARPENTARIA.

CAPE
Tribulation
COOKTOWN

CAPE
YORK
PENINSULA

BURKETOWN

CAIRNS

Rainforest
GREAT

Little
Eva crash
site

BARRIER

Gulf COUNTRY

REEF

QUEENSLAND

SIMPSON
DESERT

ce
ings

THE GREAT DIVIDING RANGE

STURT STONY
DESERT

MOUND SPRINGS
CHAMBERS CREEK
(NOW CALLED STURT
CREEK)

LAKE
TORRENS

NEW
SOUTH
WALES

ort
sta

Adelaide

Sydney

VICTORIA

Melbourne

8

Introdu

I've been to Australia many times and yet the beauty, the ruggedness, the dry, arid and empty depths of this land continue to fascinate me. The moment you turn off your car engine, there's a timeless quality, a sense of things that never change. It's a staggeringly beautiful country, with a breathtaking range of landscapes, flora and fauna, and a spiritual and cultural heritage that is both unique and deeply profound – all the more so for being still very much alive.

I've spent a lot of time with aboriginal people and am lucky that they have taught me to appreciate the Australian bush, a terrain that has defied some of the most heroic men, and imbued the natives with a heritage and a spirituality that defines their world. In the Australian outback, everyone is an explorer, and must fight for their survival, from the humble snakes and indigenous plants to the people looking to claim the land and open it to the world, and the aboriginals themselves, for whom the earth has spiritual links.

It's a harsh yet dynamic environment, and it continues to impassion me many years after I first set foot on Australia's

shores. I was inspired – no, driven – to get right into the bush: to attempt survival like so many generations of men had before me, to find a way to live off terrain that was remorselessly dry, to learn the traditions that have driven indigenous cultures for many millennia. I wanted to experience the real Australia, and to absorb the stories of the many people who had crossed her depths in years gone by.

And so, I went walkabout. Walkabout is a funny word – a word that has literally taken on a life of its own since it was first used in aboriginal culture. Once it meant an initiation ritual for a boy when he turned thirteen or thereabouts, whereby he was cast into the bush in order to earn his manhood. A walkabout could be a walk to where a man or woman originated, the land of their ancestors. Today, walkabout can relieve them of the burden of modern life, and put them back in touch with their place of sacred belongingness. In the past, many tribes used the term 'walkabout' when they went hunting, and some still do. I joked with the aboriginal people we worked with that it can also mean not turning up for work because you have a hangover (a joke at my film crew's expense). Everyone went walkabout. Everyone still does.

In aboriginal cultures, there is a tradition of walking stories from the Dreamtime when their world was created. There are sacred paths that need to be maintained, links to hallowed sites where their art, their magic, their laws and their spiritual and social history were mapped out, providing wisdom for living, and detailing the responsibilities that aboriginal tribesmen were obligated to fulfil. These could be practical things like maintaining waterholes in the desert, refreshing rock paintings, or paying respect to ancestors who they believe are still very much alive in the land; or it could be setting out along 'song lines' to sing or tell their story, to renew their faith, to satisfy spiritual demands and rituals, and to put back into the earth what she required to remain animated and energetic.

My journeys are charted throughout this book, and they are, to me, the stuff of memories that I will cherish, because I've learned, I've understood, I've met the spiritual holders of the Australian continent, and, above all, I've discovered

how to survive. There is something profound in that. Many of the first people to arrive in Australia took the view that the land would have to adapt to their way of life, but in fact you have to adapt to it, as the aboriginals did.

I've learned about the early days of Australian civilisation – as much as possible, as it is still enshrouded in mystery; I've learned about the men who staked their lives and livelihoods on finding what lay in Australia's interior and charting her coastline. I've met indigenous populations, and heard some intimate details of their culture. I've seen sacred rock art sites deep in the Australian bush, which tell stories through pictures that no one but the local aboriginals can ever relate, and then only to each other.

I've slept under the stars, and put my bushcraft skills to the test. I've encountered crocodiles and snakes, been plagued by flies and mosquitoes, experienced great thirst and sweltered in the heat, and yet still enjoyed myself. Each different part of Australia I visited had new challenges: there's rainforest, desert, scrub, rocky escarpments, marshland, sandhills and mangrove swamp. More and more, I became aware that Australia is not a country but a vast continent. In each area, the aboriginal people speak different languages and have different traditions and skills. You can no more generalise about them than you can about Europeans or Asians.

Today, most aboriginals have left the bush and moved into towns, to be near modern medical facilities, to be able to buy their food in shops rather than have to go out hunting for it, and to live a more comfortable life. Sadly, a side effect of this is that traditional skills are being lost forever. That's why it's important to record and pass on ancient wisdom, and a few people are still doing just that, such as Les Hiddins, the 'Bush Tucker Man' I travelled across Queensland with, and the family of Syd Kyle-Little, a remarkable man who used to be a policeman in the wilds of Arnhem Land.

The Australian bush offers a taste of nature at her finest and most brutal, and it provides a picture of true beauty that often masks a defiant and inhospitable spirit. My walkabout inspired me, and imbued me with knowledge that I'll carry with me forever. I hope my journey will begin to do the same for you.

The Early Explorers

Above: *William Dampier was a remarkable man, who was well ahead of his time.*

Left: *The first explorers who sighted the shores of Australia had no idea that it was an island.*

The first Europeans to land in Australia in the 17th and 18th centuries found a country that was blisteringly hot, parched dry and seemed largely empty. As they ventured on shore in their cumbersome European clothing, they came across unfamiliar plant species, huge swarms of insects, a strange hopping creature with a pouch, and occasionally some dark-skinned natives brandishing spears. But these guys who had made it down the length of the Atlantic, round the Horn of Africa and across the Indian Ocean in wooden sailing boats weren't the types to scare easily. Every one of them was a hero, and through their efforts a stunning new continent was charted.

There were dozens of expeditions to Australia, her surrounding seas, islands and straits, and into the heart of the bush, and the details have become the stuff of legend. Plaques and statues honouring these brave

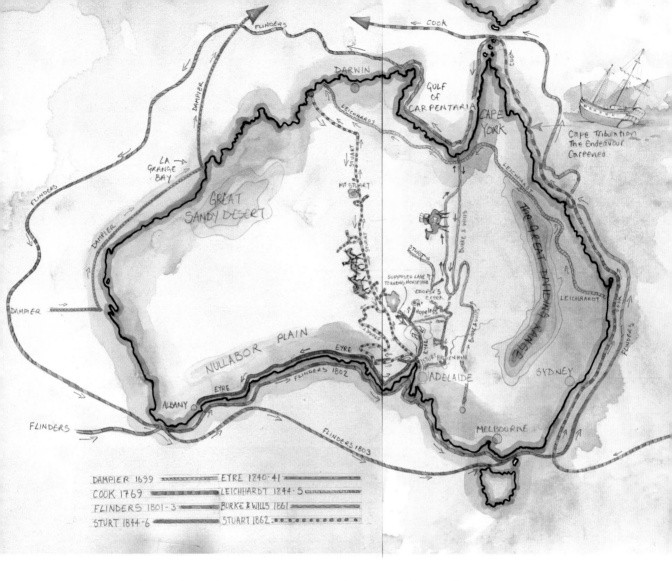

DAMPIER 1699 ✕✕✕✕✕✕✕✕✕✕ EYRE 1840-41 ━━━━━━
COOK 1769 ▬▬▬▬▬ LEICHHARDT 1844-5 ⌇⌇⌇⌇⌇⌇⌇⌇⌇
FLINDERS 1801-3 ▬▬▬ BURKE & WILLS 1861 ━━━━
STURT 1844-6 ▬▬▬ STUART 1862 ▪▪▪▪▪▪▪▪▪▪

explorers are found throughout the country, and many of the modern-day maps, road systems and charts hail from these early forays into unknown territory.

One of my favourite characters is William Dampier (1651–1715), the very first Englishman to set foot on Australian soil, and an explorer who has been largely, and unjustly, forgotten by history. Dampier was born in Somerset and began his career in the Royal Navy. He left in 1675 to take up the position of plantation manager in the West Indies and during the voyage to Jamaica he began writing a journal. After a few months in Jamaica, he headed out to sea again, living a hard and dangerous life among men who were largely buccaneers. His journals are full of exquisitely detailed descriptions of the wildlife he encountered in his journeys over the next decade. In August 1685 he transferred to the *Cygnet* where he became navigating officer under Captain Swan. They sailed across the Pacific to Guam and in January 1688 Dampier first landed in northern Australia at King Sound, or Collier Bay. He found little to commend the country, finding it no more 'fruitful' than his predecessors – such as Dutchman Abel Tasman, who had given it the name 'New Holland' after alighting there in 1644.

Dampier called himself a privateer, although 'profiteer' might be a more accurate term, as essentially he robbed his way across the world on behalf of the British nation – a perfectly acceptable way of earning a living in those days. However, anticipating the great age of botanical discovery in the 18th century, he was also a brilliant naturalist with an enquiring mind and an incredible capacity for enduring hardship.

Dampier returned to Australia eleven years later as commander of the HMS *Roebuck*, on an official voyage of 'discovery' for the British Admiralty. His journals from that trip gave the first written impressions of the flora and fauna, as well as the aboriginals, whom he described as the 'miserablest People in the world'. But his descriptions, said to be the inspiration for *Gulliver's Travels* (by Jonathan Swift, published in 1726), excited European scientists. His records of the flora in particular contained such impressive detail and accuracy that modern botanists have been able to identify all the species he was talking about. He was also responsible for bringing back to the UK the first botanical specimens from the continent, and around twenty of them still exist at Oxford University.

On that 1699 voyage, Dampier sailed via the treacherous seas off the Cape of Good Hope, which in its own right was a great feat of seamanship, and landed in Lagrange Bay in August. As with every explorer who ventured to these shores, his great preoccupations were finding enough food and fresh water, because the land didn't immediately seem to offer either. Salt-water creeks stretched far inland from the sea and wild animals seemed few and far between. Dampier made careful notes on the animals he saw, and ordered the drawing of several. He was the first to describe the dugong, calling it a manatee (it's actually a different species – the manatee is heavier and has an oval tail fluke but you can understand his mistake). The 'beasts like hungry wolves' he described were, of course, dingoes. And in noting 'a sort of racoons … have very short forelegs … but go jumping upon them …' he recorded the

Above: *Lagrange Bay, where Dampier came ashore on his second voyage to Australia.*

Below: *Dampier described termite mounds as being like 'Hottentot houses' when he viewed them through his telescope.*

wallaby. He and his fellow sailors killed sharks for food but had trouble finding sustenance from the land.

He described the shingleback lizard as a form of 'guano', sea urchins were compared to shells, and fish and birds to similar European species. One of his greatest fascinations was the termite mounds. Many parts of Australia are dominated by termite mounds, which are the most amazing feats of insect engineering. Termites mix together mud and saliva, which hardens to form a cement-like substance. They use this substance to build mounds up to 6 metres in height. A single mound can take over 50 years to complete and can contain several million residents. Seeing them from a distance, Dampier couldn't at first make out what they were and he wrote:

'When we came on the top of the Hill … we saw a plain Savannah, about a half mile from us, farther in from the Sea. There were several things like Hay-cocks, standing in

Top left: *Wild kapok is useful for firelighting and the seeds make good tinder.*

Top right: *Grewia, or dogs' balls, one of the specimens described by Dampier.*

Above: *Lollybush wood is used by aboriginals to make fires.*

the Savannah; which at a distance we thought were Houses, looking just like the Hottentot's Houses at the Cape of G. Hope, but we found them to be so many Rocks ...'

He later corrected his mistake, presumably after cutting into one.

Dampier struggled to find water in the Lagrange Bay area, so he turned and followed the coast to the north, eventually reaching what is now called the Dampier Archipelago in his honour. His search for water was still unsuccessful, and he was obliged to sail to Timor. From there, Dampier went east and reached the southern coast of New Guinea on the first day of 1700, exploring much of its western and northern coast, and discovering the Dampier Strait dividing New Guinea from New Britain. He might quite possibly have sailed on and anticipated Captain James Cook's discovery of the eastern coast of Australia, but the *Roebuck* was leaking badly. On 6 March they had to abandon ship in the Ascension Islands, but fortunately Dampier managed to save his journals and plant species and get them back home.

This was Dampier's last expedition to Australia, but his botanical works and his journals were published upon his return to England, between 1703 and 1709. Though in his earlier days a buccaneer, regarded by some writers as little better than a pirate, he was quiet and modest in manner and scientifically minded. His journals opened up the fascination of Australia to the masses, and prompted interest in further scientific investigations there. He wasn't the first to describe Australian wildlife, but despite his lack of botanical training, he is credited with being the first to publish descriptions of Australian plants.

Early explorers who glimpsed the coast of Australia back in the 15th and 16th centuries believed they were seeing a large southern landmass that extended all the way to the South Pole. When they looked at the horizon shimmering in the heat, they had no way of knowing there was another ocean between this red, dusty land and the ice shelves of Antarctica.

The quest to find the 'Southern Continent' was to bring many explorers to Australia and her surrounds. The idea of *Terra Australis Incognita* – the 'unknown land of the south' – was developed by the ancient Greeks. They theorised that if the earth was round, there surely existed a large southern landmass to balance the weight of the known world of the northern hemisphere. Maps depicted this massive assumed continent, stretching all the way to the South Pole. This idea had become controversial in Europe by the Middle Ages, when the flat-world theory held sway, but was revived in the 15th century as a new enthusiasm for exploration developed and knowledge of the southern sea increased.

Portuguese explorers Bartholomew Diaz (1450–1500) and Vasco de Gama (1460–1524) showed that Africa extended only to the Cape of Good Hope. Ferdinand Magellan (1480–1521), by entering the Pacific from the east in 1521, showed that South America was not connected to a southern continent. He died during the journey, but one of his ships managed to circumnavigate the world, proving that it was indeed round. Francis Drake (c 1540–c 1596), on his journey of 1577 to 1580, discovered the Drake Passage (between Tierra del Fuego and the south) and observed that no visible landmass existed south of Cape Horn.

The myth of *Terra Australis* persisted in spite of all these, and more expeditions were sent in search of it during the 17th and 18th centuries. Jean-Baptiste Bouver de Lozier in 1738 and Yves Joseph de Kerguelen-Termarec in 1772 discovered a few subantarctic islands and concluded that their discoveries marked the edge of a southern continent.

But even when Antarctica was discovered at the base of the Southern hemisphere, the search continued.

Captain James Cook (1728–1799) was the Englishman most famously credited with 'discovering' Australia – despite the fact that he was there almost a century after Dampier (and the fact that aboriginals had probably been there for tens of thousands of years). In 1769 he arrived on Australia's eastern shores, claiming it for Britain and changing the name from 'New Holland' to 'New South Wales'. Based on his reports of 'fine harbours for settlement' and 'grassy fields', a penal colony was set up a decade later in Botany Bay, in an attempt to 'cleanse the festering sores' of England's overflowing prisons.

Captain Cook was born in Yorkshire, and was appointed command of his first ship after only three years of apprenticeship, at the age of just twenty-

Above: *Cape Tribulation. For Cook to get a hole in his ship here, so far from home, is equivalent to a modern-day astronaut having an engine malfunction while on the moon.*

Below: *A plaque in Cooketown, where the Endeavour was careened.*

seven. A stint in the navy took him on exploratory voyages to the St Lawrence River in Canada, and he acquired a considerable knowledge of marine surveying, as well as studying mathematics and astronomy. When the Royal Society decided to send a competent observer to the South Pacific, so that the transit of Venus could be observed on 3 June 1769, Cook was promoted to lieutenant and given command of the expedition. His ship, the *Endeavour*, was only 30 metres long, but she was well fitted for her special work. There was no secret about Cook's sailing instructions in relation to the transit of Venus, but he had also received secret instructions from the admiralty to search for a southern continent, and 'take possession of convenient situations in the country in the name of the King of Great Britain'.

The *Endeavour* arrived in Tahiti in 1769, at that date the only vessel to avoid the crew being struck down with scurvy. Cook had insisted on cleanliness in the men's

quarters, and had persuaded his crew to eat sauerkraut with their salt meat, thus providing enough vitamin C to keep them healthy.

During the next six months Cook sailed completely round New Zealand and charted the coastline. He only had provisions left for four months more, and he had to decide whether he would return to Britain via Cape Horn or the Cape of Good Hope. He decided to turn to the west and make for Van Diemen's Land (now known as Tasmania) but the wind forced him to the north, and the first land he sighted was Point Hicks, near the present boundary of New South Wales and Victoria. He reached there in April 1770, and following the coast to the north came to Botany Bay a few weeks later.

Disaster struck on the night of 11 June when the *Endeavour* hit part of the Great Barrier Reef and incurred a large hole in her side. Fortunately a bit of coral remained stuck in place, plugging the hole to an extent, and they managed to limp to shore at Cape Tribulation, taking on water and listing badly. Normally, in those days, if you damaged your boat you were in serious trouble, but Cook was a brilliant seaman. They rowed further north, looking for a natural harbour where repairs could be undertaken. When they reached a bay, at the mouth of a river, Cook went ashore and climbed Grassy Hill to

Top and above: *Joseph Banks' painting of the Endeavour careened in Weary Bay, and the same scene when we filmed there in 2007. The main change is that the woods were thinner in 1770 because aboriginals used to burn back the scrub seasonally.*

plot a way in through the reefs. They brought the ship in to anchor in the mouth of the river, now known as the Endeavour River, at a place they named Weary Bay because they were so weary from rowing. A botanist called Sir Joseph Banks painted the scene with the *Endeavour* careened to one side. When I was filming the BBC series, we went there and found the exact spot and, coincidentally, there was a boat in the same place as the *Endeavour*, which was also careened to one side. The woodland today is much thicker than it was back then because aboriginal people no longer work the land and burn back vegetation in the way they used to – but otherwise it looks almost exactly the same.

Cook and his men repaired the boat and set sail again in August 1770. Cook was glad to be able to find a way outside the Great Barrier Reef and, on reaching Torres Strait, he landed again and took formal possession of the coastline before returning to Britain to report his findings – that New Zealand was not attached to a larger land mass to the south and that by charting almost the entire eastern coastline of Australia he had shown it to be continental in size. He also was the first to describe a kangaroo back home!

In 1772, he was once again commissioned by the Royal Society to search for the mythical *Terra Australis*, which they still thought lay further to the south. Cook commanded HMS *Resolution* on this voyage, while Tobias Furneaux commanded its companion ship, HMS *Adventure*. Cook's expedition circumnavigated the globe at a very southerly latitude, becoming one of the first to cross into the Antarctic Circle on 17 January 1773. He also surveyed, mapped and took possession for Britain of South Georgia, and navigated the South Sandwich Islands (Hawaiian Islands).

In the Antarctic fog, *Resolution* and *Adventure* became separated. Furneaux made his way to New Zealand, where he lost some of his men following a fight with the Maori, and eventually sailed back to Britain, while Cook continued to explore the Antarctic.

Not surprisingly, he found no *Terra Australis* and, in fact, came back with clear evidence that it was possible to sail around the Antarctic and that the largest land mass above it was Australia itself.

Top: *Benjamin Herschel Babbage found a way to get through the Lake Torrens 'horseshoe'.*

Top: *Edward John Eyre crossed Southern Australia from east to west.*

An Englishman, Matthew Flinders (1774–1814), was the first man to circumnavigate Australia and his charts of the coast were to prove so accurate that some are still in use in the 21st century. While sailing with the famous Captain Bligh (of *Mutiny on the Bounty* fame) on a boat called the *Providence*, he charted part of the south-east coast of Tasmania and many small islands, mainly in the Fiji group. Bligh was impressed with Flinders' ability and entrusted the young man with chart-making and astronomical observations and the care of the precious and incredibly important time-keepers on board. It was on the *Providence* that Flinders first caught sight of Australia and his passion for discovery was aroused.

Before long, in 1798 he was back in Australian waters aboard the *Reliance*. He became friendly with British ship's doctor George Bass (1771–1803), and they teamed up to make many exploratory journeys along the Australian coast together. Flinders had prepared well for his journey, buying a tiny 2-metre boat dubbed 'Tom Thumb', in which Bass, Flinders and his assistant William Martin could chart the coastal inlets and rivers in the Port Jackson area. Smugglers were the best boat-builders in those days, and Deal in Kent was a favoured boat yard where Captains Cook and Bligh, among others, got the boats for their historic voyages.

It was difficult work, combatting rough seas, high winds and nervous aboriginals. In a larger boat, the *Norfolk*, they proved that Tasmania was an island, separated by a strait which was then named in honour of Bass. Bass also began to write a detailed 'Natural History' and attempt a study of the Tasmanian aboriginals. But this was the last voyage Bass and Flinders undertook together, as Bass mysteriously vanished somewhere in the Pacific in 1803. Meanwhile, in 1802, Flinders was asked by the British government to circumnavigate Australia. He sailed north from Sydney in the *Investigator*, passed through the Torres Strait and across the Gulf of Carpentaria. He had the wisdom on this trip to recruit two aboriginals – named Bungaree and Nanbaree – to accompany him and help him to trade with local tribes for food and water. As we'll see with later inland explorers, this made all the difference in such inhospitable terrain, and most of the successful Australian adventurers would do the same thing. Flinders' visit to Arnhem Land is recorded in some paintings of European ships at rock art sites in the region. The voyage was a huge success and by the end he had charted the entire coastline of Australia, linking together other partial surveys to give the first complete picture.

Above: *Edmund Kennedy was killed by hostile aboriginals on the Cape York peninsula.*

It was Flinders who gave the name 'Australia' to the country. He wrote to his brother: 'I call the whole island Australia, or Terra Australis.' And later that year he corresponded with Sir Joseph Banks, mentioning 'my general chart of Australia'. He continued to promote the name but could not convince Banks to endorse it. As a result, Flinders' book was published under the title *A Voyage to Terra Australis*. The day after it was published in 1814, he died, aged only 40, but he had already forged for himself an indelible place in Australian history.

Above: *Matthew Flinders made such accurate charts of the Australian coast that they were used for generations after his death.*

When the English first started to colonise Australia in the decades after 1788, little was known about the land. These were white-skinned seamen in shirts, trousers and boots, who were ill prepared for the intensity of the sun, the ferocity of the biting insects and, worst of all, the lack of fresh water. The biggest problem of all was always going to be water.

The flora, the fauna, the temperature, the climate were just so different from back home. In the southern part of Australia there are temperate regions but as you move into the middle there are more or less three seasons – the dry season, the build-up season and the rainy season. It was the sheer scale of the country that was staggering to the first explorers to venture beyond the coast. They were sent north and south along the coast, and west into the inland, seeking to cross the Great Dividing Range to find sources of fresh water, sites for other settlements and suitable land for grazing sheep and farming. This exploration posed monumental challenges – and many of them never returned.

Successful inland explorers were few and far between. Just a day in the Australian bush provides ample evidence of why. This is beautiful country, but many parts remain inhospitable and dangerous. Even modern-day aboriginals have moved their settlements away from the bush's depths, where survival is still only possible for the fittest and the best equipped. Skill and instinct played a huge part in the survival of the earliest explorers, and many were to come to a sad end in the vast, uncharted land.

In 1827, Englishman Charles Sturt arrived in New South Wales and began exploring the Macquarie, Lachlan, Murrumbidgee, Darling and Murray river system. At the time, it was believed that there must be a massive ocean or lake in the centre of Australia because so many rivers seemed to lead inland. Although nervous of aboriginals he met on his travels, he treated them with kindness and even befriended some, and he soon discovered that they were only trying to scare away the invaders rather than slaughter them. Sturt's approach meant that they offered him invaluable assistance on his journey and helped him to make peace with other tribes he met subsequently. Before long, Sturt had discovered the lower reaches of the Darling River, which was in full flow, enabling him to prove that all the rivers that flowed west eventually turned south to the ocean and there was no inland sea.

Sturt's journey was fraught with problems finding food and water for his party, and most of his men suffered from severe exhaustion. Vitamin deficiency robbed him of his eyesight for several months but he was compensated on his return to England in 1834 when he was given 50,000 acres of land near Mittagong in New South Wales. It was because of his explorations that the city of Adelaide was settled. In 1838, Sturt made another famous overland trek from Sydney to Adelaide, taking a herd of much-needed cattle. This time the journey took just 40 days and enabled him to prove that the Hume and the Murray were one and the same river. He settled in South Australia and was appointed surveyor general and later registrar general.

Sturt's last major expedition began in 1844, when he was almost 50 years of age, when he decided to try to reach the centre of the country. Early in the trip he was confronted by hostile aboriginals, but managed to reason with them. The party passed through today's Broken Hill, but failed to recognise the valuable minerals in the ground. Further north, at Rocky Glen (near the present town of Milparinka), they were trapped for six months by the extreme heat and the lack of water in the terrain ahead. The party came down with scurvy because of the lack of fresh food, and a number of them died. Despite being very near to the centre of the country, Sturt was forced to turn back, as his sight once again failed. The heat was so intense that rivers were bone dry, screws fell out of boxes as the wood rotted, and thermometers shattered. When the winter arrived again, the bitter cold caused frostbite and chilblains – all in the same landscape.

One final expedition, with three men, also ended in failure; however, Sturt had found a route to the centre of Australia. His explorations added much to the current knowledge of the Australian interior, but he just couldn't solve the one problem that held him back from achieving his goal – water.

Edward John Eyre (1815–1901) came to Australia at the age of seventeen, hoping to make his fortune by combining sheep and cattle droving with a bit of exploration. Together with his aboriginal friend Wylie, he trekked across the Nullarbor Plain from Adelaide to Albany, becoming the first white man to cross southern Australia from east to west. Along the way he was looking out for good sheep and cattle grazing and droving routes, and he paved the way for the settlement of much of southern Australia.

Unable to resist the big challenge of the day, Eyre set out in 1839 to reach the centre of Australia, with a view to opening up a route that could be used

by settlers – but he found himself blocked by swamps and sandhills, so turned back and switched his attentions to the southern route.

Eyre's party for the crossing from Adelaide in 1840 was composed of six white men, three aboriginals, thirteen horses, 40 sheep and supplies to last them all three months. Soon the harsh conditions and lack of water on what is now known as Eyre Peninsula forced Eyre to send everyone back to Adelaide, except for Baxter (his sheep station manager) and the three aboriginals. He reasoned that a smaller party might have more chance of success. Their route from Fowler's Bay across the Nullarbor Plain was 1,300 kilometres long and was defined throughout by their desperate search for water. Some local aboriginals showed Eyre how to find water by digging behind the sand dunes on the seashore, how to break off the roots of gum trees and suck them to relieve their thirst, to collect early morning dew from leaves and to recognise, use and look after native wells and waterholes.

Wylie proved his loyalty to Eyre by raising the alarm when the two other aboriginals in their party plundered the stores and killed Baxter. The aboriginals disappeared, leaving Eyre and Wylie on their own and without food, but they survived by killing and eating kangaroos. In June 1841, they came upon a French whaling ship anchored off the coast at Rossiter Bay where they rested for two weeks before reaching Albany in July. Their journey had lasted four and a half months.

Eyre was awarded a gold medal of the Royal Geographical Society for this incredible journey and in 1846, he was made Lieutenant-Governor of New Zealand before retiring to England, where he lived until his death in 1901. Wylie was rewarded with a pension, and he remained in Albany, amongst his own people.

Left: *The Great Sandy Desert of Western Australia has average daytime temperatures of 38 to 42°C in summer but the rainfall is quite high for a desert, with 250 to 300mm a year.*

Eyre's friendship with an aboriginal saved his life on many occasions but another Englishman, Edmund Kennedy (1818–1848), was not so fortunate. He made many expeditions into unexplored areas of Queensland, opening up several new areas, before being speared to death while trying to find a route to the tip of the Cape York Peninsula.

Kennedy arrived in Sydney in 1840, and in 1845, he was second-in-command of an expedition led by Thomas Mitchell, on which they discovered the Victoria River and rich grasslands in central Queensland. On another expedition in 1847, Kennedy discovered that the Victoria River did not flow into the Gulf as Mitchell had thought, but was part of Cooper's Creek. He renamed it the Barcoo River.

In 1848, Kennedy, together with twelve other men, left Rockingham Bay north of Townsville to travel to Cape York. The journey was overwhelmingly difficult, through thick jungle and mangrove swamps backed by mountains, drenched by late tropical rains and pursued by hostile aboriginals who trailed the party for hundreds of miles. Their horses died and the party became increasingly weak when they failed to trap or find sufficient food. They reached Weymouth Bay six months later, where they established a depot.

Kennedy and four others left the depot to try and reach Cape York, where they knew a relief ship was expected. However, as the party got smaller, the aboriginals who had been following them decided to attack. When they were just 20 kilometres from Cape York, Kennedy was speared and killed. At the Weymouth Bay depot, only two survivors were found.

A few years after Kennedy's death, another intrepid spirit in the form of Benjamin Herschel Babbage (1815–1878), an engineer, scientist and explorer who was born in London, set out to make his mark. In 1851, Babbage was appointed by the South Australian government to make a 'Geological and Mineralogical Survey' of the colony. In 1856 he was sent north to search for gold as far as the Flinders Ranges. He found none, but discovered the MacDonnell River, Blanchewater and Mount Hopeful. At the time it was thought that there was a horseshoe-shaped saltpan, known as Lake Torrens, encircling the Flinders Range and blocking any path to the interior. Babbage was the first to dispel this idea by ascertaining the existence of a north-east gap through to the Cooper and Gulf Country.

Babbage left in February 1858 to explore the country between Lakes Torrens and Gairdner, and further to the north and west. He was slow and methodical, which angered the government, who wanted to open the country for colonisation and to find any potentially lucrative resources as quickly as possible. He was, therefore, relieved by Peter Warburton (1813–1889). After his experiences of 1856, Babbage was keen to cross through the gap in the Lake Torrens 'horseshoe' and at Hermit Hill he did so, but Warburton was the first to traverse it completely. It is Warburton whose name is now synonymous with the exploration of Western Australia, while Babbage remains an unsung hero who once described himself as a 'gentleman', with 'scientific qualifications of a high order which are not easily found combined in one man'.

Throughout the 19th century, acting on rumours that there were rivers and a great lake in the centre of the continent, explorers continued to venture into the interior – but most of these expeditions foundered in the hostile environment. They knew there was a huge economic potential if they could find gold or minerals worth mining, or grazing land for sheep and cattle, but few actually succeeded.

Among those few was Augustus Charles Gregory (1819–1905), an assistant surveyor who was well known for his bushcraft skills. In 1846 he commanded an expedition north of Perth, mapping the Gascoigne River, the Murchison River and the Champion Bay district. In 1855 he sailed from Queensland to Victoria and mapped the Victoria River. There is a boab tree named 'Gregory's Tree' in his honour that is now registered as a Sacred Site of significance to local Ngaringman people.

Sir John Forrest (1847–1918) won fame as an explorer by leading three expeditions into the interior of Western Australia. He was appointed Surveyor General and in 1890 became the first Premier of Western Australia, its only premier as a self-governing colony. In March 1869 he led an expedition from Perth in search of clues to the fate of the explorer Leichhardt. Ludwig Leichhardt was a German explorer and scientist who came to Australia in 1842 to study its rocks and wildlife, perhaps inspired by Dampier's work. He had led an expedition to find a new route to Port Essington, near Darwin. Leichhardt left the Darling Downs in October 1844, and after a perilous journey of fifteen months and over 5,000 kilometres, his party finally reached Port Essington.

They named the Dawson, Mackenzie, Isaacs, Suttor and Burdekin Rivers, as well as Expedition Range and Peak Range. On a journey from Moreton Bay to Perth, his party disappeared. Many reasons, from mutiny to floods, have been suggested as explanations for their disappearance, but it still remains a mystery today. Leichhardt's expedition and disappearance inspired Patrick White to base his great novel *Voss* on the explorer.

Determined to uncover the cause of Leichhardt's disappearance, Forrest led six men and sixteen horses over 3,200 kilometres inland, almost as far as the site later known as Laverton. While he found neither Leichhardt nor any good pastoral land, Forrest systematically surveyed his route using the most up-to-date methods of stellar observation, and he brought back specimens for botanists and geologists. Forrest and his brother Alexander later surveyed the route between Western Australia and South Australia taken 30 years earlier by Eyre.

Forrest and Gregory had the skills and the resources they needed to tackle the inhospitable land, and called upon the successful strategies of their forebears, along with current science, to complete their journeys. But not everyone was as well organised, or as careful. The explorers Burke and Wills undertook a calamitous journey in 1860–1 that was emblematic of poor planning and leadership, as well as a resounding reminder of the dangers of the Australian bush.

Robert O'Hara Burke (1821–1861) and William John Wills (1834–1861) were both English-born and emigrated to Australia, where they were to make their names as the first colonists to traverse the continent from south to north. Their 1860 journey of exploration was the largest and most costly ever mounted in Australia at the time. It was also one of the most appalling failures, and many of the party needlessly lost their lives.

Burke headed the expedition, but he was an impatient man with questionable leadership and decision-making skills, and was arrogant enough to believe that he knew best, even when provided with evidence to the contrary from more experienced or knowledgeable members of his party. He had little if any bushcraft knowledge, which was to flaw the expedition from the outset. In 1860, Burke and Wills travelled from Melbourne to the Gulf of Carpentaria, along with a huge entourage of 28 horses and wagons, 24 camels, two years' supply of food and almost 6 tons of firewood. Their procession ran for more than half a kilometre. Among their equipment, they carried 120 mirrors as gifts for the natives, 60 gallons of rum, 4 gallons of brandy, supplies of rockets, arms and vast quantities of dried foods.

One of Burke's first mistakes was to ignore warnings about the heat of summer and set off from Melbourne at completely the wrong time of year. Infuriated with the delays associated with such a huge party, he divided it at Menindee, some 700 kilometres north, and took eight men on to the halfway point at Cooper's Creek. There he waited for six weeks for the others to catch up.

En route they managed to alarm local aboriginals, who were concerned about the damage to their waterholes caused by the horses and camels. Some waterholes only hold a few litres – plenty for a man to quench his thirst, but a volume that can be drained by a horse in one go. What's more, Burke decided he didn't need any help from aboriginals at all and refused to trade with them, so he didn't get the benefits of any of their expertise.

Burke's objective of reaching the Gulf of Carpentaria was successful, but it was a dramatic and difficult journey. He fell out with many members of his party, and ended up making the final 1000-kilometre dash with only Wills and two other men. Team member William Brahe was left at Cooper's Creek in charge of a small group, with instructions not to leave unless absolutely necessary.

Burke and Wills left Cooper's Creek on 16 December with six camels and one horse, and on 9 February 1861 found themselves almost on the shore of the Gulf of Carpentaria. Through heat, desert and bog they had trekked for two months before being stopped by mangroves. The ground was too swampy to enable them to actually reach the shore, but they were close enough to be able to claim that the continent had been crossed. Wills kept a diary and it is because of this that we know what occurred next.

On 13 February they began the return journey, but wet weather made progress very slow at first and the animals gradually became weaker and weaker. One man fell ill and died about four days before the party reached Cooper's Creek on 21 April. They got there to find that Brahe and his men had

Walker's Tree

Walker marked a tree FW/12 Jan/1862 and that tree is the feature of the site now and is the sole focus of tourist attention. It is generally thought to be the Burke and Wills tree. Walker noted that this camp was about three quarters of a mile from his camp where they had been based for about four days.

Artifacts were found at Camp 119 by the staff of Magowra Station in later years buried in a Camp Oven. The artifacts included a Mercury Artificial Horizon used by Wills for his astronomical observations. I believe that the only way the staff could have found this equipment was for it to have been accidentally exposed. This would only have been possible by the bank of the lagoon having been slowly eroded out by cattle drinking at the water's edge.

Walker's failure to find the oven was because he dug 14 yards, 14 feet and 14 inches from the tree marked SSE 14. He did not realise that Surveyors used Links as a unit of measurement and not yards, feet or inches. 14 links equals 9' 3". We can deduce with a high degree of certainty that the tree was Thomson's no 13.
David Hillan, Surveyor

Left and above: *Burke and Wills cut the bark off several trees and carved their initials in the hardwood. The photograph on the left shows a tree that they marked and above there is a notice explaining the significance of another tree.*

Following pages: *The Great Sandy Desert. Peter Warburton was the first European to cross it, in 1873.*

left on the morning of that very day. Wills wished to take the track towards Menindee, which would have been by far the better course, but Burke insisted that they head south-west. It was a huge mistake and they soon became stranded, too weak to complete the trip back.

Burke, Wills and King, the other remaining team member, lived for some time on locally stored nardoo seed, gradually becoming weaker. They shunned help from local aboriginals, so Burke never realised that the nardoo, if not prepared correctly, is toxic. The seeds have to be processed to remove a chemical that depletes the body of thiamine (vitamin B1). Without thiamine, energy resources can't be metabolised properly, and gradual starvation occurs. Ironically, Burke was also unaware that the waterholes by which they made their camp were actually full of fish that they could have eaten to stay alive. Starvation set in, and Burke and Wills died at the end of June 1861.

Wills' last journal entry reads:

'Starvation on nardoo is by no means very unpleasant, but for the weakness one feels, and the utter inability to move oneself, for as far as appetite is concerned, it gives me the greatest satisfaction. Certainly, fat and sugar would be more to one's taste, in fact, those seem to me to be the great stand by for one in this extraordinary continent; not that I mean to depreciate the farinaceous food, but the want of sugar and fat in all substances attainable here is so great that they become almost valueless to us as articles of food, without the addition of something else.'

King was not so stubborn. He befriended some aboriginals, who gave him food and shelter until he was rescued by the relief party.

At the same time as the Burke and Wills expedition, one of my favourite heroes was making the same journey, albeit at a different pace and with an entirely different approach. John McDouall Stuart (1815–1866) was a remarkable man who made numerous expeditions in the Australian desert, learning more about the terrain every time. Each was training for the final one, during which he crossed the continent, establishing a route for the Overland Telegraph from Adelaide to the north coast, which would connect Australia with the rest of the world. Unlike Burke and Wills, he chose to travel light with only a couple of spare horses, and to travel fast, covering about 40 kilometres a day.

A Scotsman by birth, he arrived in South Australia in 1838 where he entered the government survey department. In 1844 he gained invaluable experience as a draughtsman on the expedition to the centre of Australia led by Captain Charles Sturt.

Stuart went on to lead six expeditions to the interior, and was the first European to 'gaze upon her red centre'. His journeys opened up thousands of valuable acres of sheep country and, despite chronic difficulties, he eventually became the first man to cross the continent from south to north and then back again. His ability to find water in the most arid situations, his persistence, courage and common sense, plus the instinct of a natural bushman were the real reasons for his success.

There's more about Stuart's methods in the Into the Desert chapter, where I describe how I traced his steps around the desert and learned more about his survival techniques. Stuart had realised early on that if he and his team were to conquer the continent, they would have to capitalise on the sources of water he was able to map on his earlier expeditions. This would ultimately result in a longer journey, but would give him and his team a much better chance of accomplishing it alive. Their meagre rations of dried meat and flour did cause severe health problems, including scurvy. Crippled and nearly blind, Stuart still led his party on the 3400-kilometre return journey. It was one of the greatest feats of survival in the history of exploration.

On the return journey, he didn't think he was going to make it. A journal entry for 18 October 1862 read: *'I have kept Nash and King with me in case of dying during the night, as it would be lonely for one young man to be there by himself. Wind south-east.'* However, they were discovered by some hands on a Mount Margaret sheep run, who later described 'ten gaunt and ragged men, one of them carried on a litter, heading a string of limping, emaciated horses, come riding slowly, wearily, triumphantly out of the mirage that filled the empty north.'

In 1863, on the same day as the remains of Burke and Wills passed on their way to burial in Melbourne, crowds lined the streets of Adelaide to welcome home a living skeleton of a man and his triumphant team. Not one of his party had died, and Stuart had refused to be awed by a vast and alien interior that had claimed so many lives and wrung dry the hopes of so many men. To him, the bush was 'wonderful country … scarcely to be believed'.

Stuart was the first man since David Livingstone to win honours from the Royal Geographical Society twice. And in his wake, right through the centre of the continent, followed the Overland Telegraph, the railway and a highway, aptly named the Stuart Highway.

In reality, however, every man who attempted to explore this vibrant yet treacherous land was heroic. Through their efforts, a continent, its extremities, interior and waterways, was discovered – a continent that I still consider one of the most stunning and dramatic places on earth. Following the journeys of some of these men has been a truly remarkable and humbling process. Traditional knowledge may be dying, but the inspirational stories of those who found their way through this unforgiving country, and had the determination to open it to others, may finally lead to its renaissance.

Every one of these explorers experienced extreme hardship and were faced with what D.H. Lawrence, during his travels to Australia in 1922, termed the land's 'lost, weary aloofness' – whether it was the impenetrable mountains, huge stretches of desert, oppressive heat, ruthless jungle and swamps, or the teeming insects of Australia. The efforts and sacrifices of these brave and sometimes foolhardy men paved the way for colonisation and opened up 'down under' to reveal a whole new world.

Syd Kyle-Little

Syd Kyle-Little's adventures, his friendship with the aboriginal people of the Northern Territory, and his bushtracking skills have become part of the fabric of Australia's history. I was honoured while filming the *Walkabout* series to meet a man who has become both a hero to white Australians and one of the staunchest defenders of the aboriginal population. There can be no white man on earth who knows the aboriginals better than Syd, and he relates his encounters with them, respectfully and free of any condescension, in his book, *Whispering Wind*.

Syd's grandfather was a British army officer, who married an Irish girl he met in Sydney in 1867 before he was posted to the Northern Territory as a policeman. Syd's father was also a policeman, responsible for patrolling the Cape York area from Laura, a small town at the end of the Overland Telegraph. Syd was born in Darwin in 1918 and, although he was educated at Brisbane on the south-east coast, he couldn't wait to get back up north. He joined the 'Permanent

Previous pages: *Syd with Narlebar, Oondabund and another patrol boy in the Liverpool River.*

Left: *Syd and me in July 2007. It was a real privilege to meet him.*

Military Force' at the age of eighteen and in 1938 he was posted to Darwin.

As a young man, before the war, Syd had spent school holidays with his uncle George Goodman, a buffalo shooter at Humpty Doo Station, a small town just south of the Arnhem Highway, approximately 40 kilometres from Darwin. There, Syd learned to shoot buffalo from horseback, befriended the native children, and began to master some of the techniques that would help him survive the bush in years to come.

After the war Syd became a Patrol Officer with the Native Affairs department, where he continued the Kyle-Little family's long association with aboriginal people, which was quite unprecedented in its day. Even in the 21st century you won't find many white Australians who have aboriginal friends; they tend to lead quite separate lives.

Between 1946 and 1950 Syd made several excursions from Darwin and Maningrida into central Arnhem Land, including two attempts to cross the Arnhem Land escarpment from north to south. The escarpment – a vast sandstone plateau, known as Stone Country – was once criss-crossed by ancient hunting and travelling routes and inhabited by many families who availed themselves of the natural rock shelters. Today, this country is rarely visited, and there are vast tracts of land that have not been stepped on by a human being for centuries. Known to aboriginal people as 'Debil-debil' country, it's not really a place for human beings.

You have to realise that Arnhem Land was a real wild frontier in the days when Syd worked there. It still is, to an extent. It's certainly very different from other parts of Australia, like a separate country in which time has stood still. It's very difficult to travel through because the roads

Right: *One of the things that made Syd special was the straight way he dealt with local people. He was a man of his word and quickly earned their respect.*

are in poor condition and there are lots of swamps and rivers to cross. In some parts, there was a strong belief in witchcraft. People who went to the toilet in the bush would hide or burn their faeces so a witch doctor couldn't get hold of it and cast a spell on them. There were all sorts of strange traditions, some of which I'm sure continue to this day. When Syd went there, he was warned that there was still cannibalism among some of the tribes. He says: 'The Liverpool River natives did not kill men for food. They ate human flesh largely from superstitious beliefs. If they killed a worthy man in battle, they ate his heart, believing they would inherit his valour and power … If they killed a fast runner, they ate part of his legs, hoping thereby to acquire his speed.'

The greatest challenge to Syd's authority was a witch doctor called Mahrdei, but the two men eventually developed a mutual respect. As Syd says in *Whispering Wind*: 'I realized that I would have to face up to Mahrdei. He was the real power here, and though I had hated him when he taunted me … – God, how I had hated him – he was a man in man's land.' Mahrdei tested Syd by challenging him to travel like an aboriginal without clothes, and without his bedding roll, which he had left on the boat. Syd passed all the tests and eventually over time Mahrdei came to respect and help him.

In *Whispering Wind*, Syd tells a story of Mahrdei performing a ceremony in which he appealed to all aboriginal spirits who had entered the bodies of crocodiles. He says: 'There were more crocodiles than I had ever seen in one place. I didn't count them. I didn't try. But I swear there were at least forty … Mahrdei, talking very softly and quietly and addressing the crocodiles by their names, walked slowly toward the water … And then he swam and the crocodiles were all around him. How could a man swim in this and survive?' After he came out unscathed, Mahrdei walked up to Syd and pointed to the water, inviting him to do the same, before laughing uproariously at his own joke. 'The balander does not swim with crocodiles,' he shouted to the assembled tribesmen, who found this extremely funny. *Balander* is their term for 'white man'.

As late as 1950, the Stone Country of Arnhem Land was represented by a large blank space on the map. It was into this land that Syd led many of his expeditions and, having been to this rugged, arid place, I find it truly

remarkable that anyone could negotiate the landscape and survive. In his book, he relates tales of floods and droughts, expeditions marred by bureaucratic infighting, terrifying crocodile attacks, charging buffalo bulls, and a very real struggle to survive in an inhospitable and completely dry land. It's all told with a deadpan, undramatic style that is very engaging, and there are lots of survival tips, such as the following: 'Crocodile … is poor food. The flesh is white, oily and tasteless … The top

of the tail is the only edible part … It produces a singularly unpleasant body odour in all those who have eaten it; and thus, except when we were really hungry, crocodile did not appear on the menu.'

His respect for the indigenous population shines through the pages of his book, and he describes the bravery and skill of the natives in dramatic, life-threatening situations with something near to awe. As a policeman, his style was firm but friendly. I think he got the balance right, although part of his authority surely came from the knowledge that he was a remarkably good shot, and if you got shot in Arnhem Land, without nearby medical care, that meant you were as good as dead. European-style hospitals and doctors hadn't made it up there. When Syd injured his foot clambering through mangrove swamps and it became badly infected, he put it in the river and let the fish nibble away the infected tissue. If he hadn't done that, he could have lost the foot to gangrene and it could easily have been fatal.

Syd made an effort to understand the aboriginal culture, beliefs and language, and has, since the 1950s, fought hard to defend their rights. His efforts to found a trading post on the coast of the Arafura Sea in the years immediately following the Second World War met with failure, although he did, with Jack Doolan, establish a post at Maningrida, where artwork was traded for supplies. The aboriginal community of Maningrida, on the traditional lands of Kunibídji people, was created as a permanent settlement by the Welfare Branch of the Northern Territory Administration in 1957.

I had been to Arnhem Land before, working with aboriginals, and Syd and I knew some of the same people and places, so when I went to meet him in July 2007, we got on very well. We had lots of things in common to talk about, a strong sense of shared recognition, and I liked him straight away. He had a look in his eyes that told of his special inner strength – a look I've only rarely come across. He was a remarkable guy, and a fine example of the British concept that you take law to a lawless place – but it's one law for all. He had a strong sense of fair play.

No one can tell his heroic story better than Syd himself. Here's what he had to say to me:

Ray Mears (RM): Tell me a little bit about your background: how did your interest in the outback start off?

Syd Kyle-Little (SK): My family – my grandfather and my father – were always in the outback. My father was a policeman who was posted to the bush outstations. When I went to school in Queensland, or in Brisbane, I always wanted to go back up to Arnhem Land. I'd read a little bit about it; my dad told me a little bit about it. He rode the Cape York area on horseback from Laura all the way up to the Cape doing surveys of the aboriginal tribes. He had a great respect for the people.

RM: Today Arnhem Land is a remote part of Australia. How was it back then?

Below: *Syd's boat, the Amity. He almost lost his life in it when it hadn't been moored with sufficient anchor chain and the tide changed.*

SK: Still remote, very few people have ever been into Arnhem Land. It's a vast piece of country

– high, extremely rough, and very hard to walk through. It's almost a series of gullies and allies. The big trouble is that you've got to find fresh water every day. Of course you can have a water bottle with you – and you can go two days without water. But if you haven't found water by then, you've got to walk back two days. So I had a rule, something I've always abided by: if I hadn't found water on the second day, I'd turn back, regardless. By the time you got back, after four days of no water, your mouth was so dry, it was incredible. Two days out, and two days back.

RM: Part of the reason for the land being so dry is that the tidal reach is so huge, there are massive tides there.

SK: Arnhem Land is too far in. The tidal reach is great. It pushes the fresh water back up the rivers into the interior, and the rivers split up into little creeks. When they come up towards the escarpment, they're just little tiny creeks and in the dry season, they all dry up. There's very little water left anywhere. After you cross the escarpment and start to move south, there really is no water, and you've got to be very, very careful.

RM: The first time you went into Arnhem Land, you didn't know this, did you? Tell me about that.

SK: I was Cadet Patrol Officer in Darwin, and we were given a letter by the Northern Territory Administrator. Some missionaries complained that there were two murderers on the loose.

Above: *Oondabund, Syd's trusty friend, was a tracker who worked with him for many years.*

Above: *Syd on mounted patrol as a Patrol Officer with the Native Affairs department.*

So I went out on my own, by lugger [a kind of boat] to Entrance Island at the mouth of the Liverpool River and I went ashore. I spoke to the tribes there, and I picked up two aboriginals called Oondabund and Narlebar [as guides]. I said, 'You know these murderers?' They said 'Yes'. I said, 'Will you come with me and tell me where they are?' They said, 'Yes, we'll show you, we know where they are.'

RM: When you got dropped off by the lugger, did you have your equipment?

SK: In all the rush, the captain of the lugger, who was a missionary taking his stuff off as well, was standing by me. We got into the canoe to go ashore, and as we were coming in I suddenly realised that I'd left all my fags, my swag, and all my food back on the ship. And there she is, sailing merrily away, and I'm in a dugout canoe, with two aboriginals and nothing else. I thought: *Bloody hell*, what am I going to do? So we paddled ashore. They said, 'No matter, boss, we'll get bush tucker.' So that was really the first time I started to live on bush tucker. I ate wallaby and all sorts of things.

RM: Has that influenced your relationship with aboriginal people?

SK: Oh yes, but my relationship with aboriginals started when I was a boy. Back when we used to run a place called Humpty Doo, I used to go up there for school holidays, and there were aboriginal boys out there. They used to take me out. They taught me a hell of a lot, how to track, lots of things – and it was good fun.

RM: And how important would you say tracking is in the bush?

SK: If you want to survive, you've got to be able to track, simple as that.

RM: But it's a skill that's disappearing now, isn't it?

SK: Very few people can track – very few aboriginals these days can track. If they want something they go to the local store and buy it. But who pays them? The government. They're losing all their traditional skills.

RM: So there you were, dropped off in Arnhem Land, and you are effectively representing the authority of the Australian government.

Below: *Syd with some of his trackers. They have traditional scarification markings, into which they rubbed ash, and they are carrying woomera, or spear throwers. I have hunted with woomera but it's a skill that is fast disappearing today.*

SK: That's right.

RM: To collect two murderers, who were aboriginals living out there among their friends …

SK: Yeah.

RM: And you haven't got your equipment?

SK: That's right.

RM: That's a pretty scary situation.

SK: Well, there was nothing I could do about it. I had my two aboriginals, and I said, 'Can we catch these fellows?' They said, 'Yeah, we can catch them alright.' I asked when we were going to get them, and one of them looked at the other, and said, 'Look, you catch them when the sun comes up, early morning. Those fellows wait up all night for you to come and catch them, and when you don't turn up, they go to sleep by the fire.' Sure enough, they tracked them right up to where they had their fire, and they were both asleep. I walked in and said, 'Good morning gentlemen'. I had a 303 rifle, and I said, 'Who wants to run?' They looked a bit horrified.

RM: You didn't use handcuffs, did you?

SK: No, I never, ever used handcuffs or chains, and I couldn't see the point of using them. I used to say to them, 'If you want to run, I might not kill you. I'll just blow your ankle out, or blow your kneecap off.' And they said, 'Oh, that's worse than being killed.' I never did it to anybody, but the threat of doing it put the fear of god in them.

Left: *Arnhem Land aboriginals used mud or ochre to paint their faces for traditional ceremonies.*

RM: When I read what you wrote about your experiences there [in *Whispering Wind*], one of the things I thought was very interesting was your faith in their code of honour.

SK: Yes, they've got a code of honour that's in many ways better than ours. They stand by their code of honour, every inch of the way. If they say they're going to do something, maybe they say they're going to kill somebody, they kill them. They don't bug about. They've got an excellent code of honour.

RM: And you relied upon that, didn't you?

SK: I did. That's how I got the two murderers. I said, 'No handcuffs, no chains', and they looked at me. I said, 'You promise me you won't run away, because if you run away, I promise *you*, you'll never be able to walk again, and I'll leave you here, and you'll die a slow death. All the ants can eat you.' I never really had any trouble. They understood me, and I understood them.

RM: I think it's very interesting that you also had to prove yourself. Wasn't there one occasion where you actually ended up having a boxing match with one of the aboriginals?

SK: It wasn't boxing as such – it was an order of wrestling and boxing, bite, kick, bite, everything else, rolling on the ground.

RM: How did that come about?

SK: They said that white men can't fight. I didn't want to fight, but I was standing there, with two tribes and about 300 people watching. They said things like 'Oh, you clever man, you've got a rifle, but we've got no rifles'. I said, 'Fine, take my rifle'. And they said, 'Right, you want to fight now?' I told them I had no spears, they had my rifle, how did they want to fight? One of them jumped in, and he said, 'I'll fight you', and he jumped at me like a kangaroo, knocked me head over tail on the ground. I stood up, and thought: *Holy mackerel*, what have I got myself into? And he knocked me down again. I sort of heard the mob cheering – they were shouting and screaming. I thought it had been rigged. I got off my knees again, and then he came roaring in like an express train, and I swung a punch, right hand of course, and hit him in the jaw, and knocked him head over turkey on the ground. He got up again, and I got up, and I whacked him again, and it went on for about five minutes. In the end, he said, 'I'm finished, boss. No more, please, no more. I'm finished. You can win.'

RM: Didn't you feel at all isolated? There you are, a solitary white man in this remote part of Australia, surrounded by people who are used to using spears, people who are quite warlike?

Below: *Song and dance are part of many traditional ceremonies.*

SK: No, I believed in their code of honour. They said they'd accept me because, for one thing, I didn't use handcuffs and chains. They said to me, 'Where are your irons, your handcuffs, your chains?' I said, 'I don't need them because I trust you.' So they learned to take my word; they used to refer to me as 'the man' – the balander.

RM: This must have been quite unusual at that time – it wasn't the normal white attitude to dealing with the natives.

SK: No, it wasn't, most of the police used to handcuff and chain them, round the neck, all to make it so they couldn't walk. I couldn't see the sense in that, when they're out in the bush. I took a man's word of honour. I went to the trouble of learning a bit about their language, and I can understand a little bit about them.

RM: That must've been very difficult.

SK: Oh, it was difficult. I was on my own. It was very difficult.

RM: My experience of Arnhem Land is that there are so many languages.

SK: The big tribes are the most important ones, that's the only thing that I bothered to learn. And I did learn a great deal about them – just understanding. I've probably forgotten everything I ever learnt, 40 years later.

RM: In my own experience of Arnhem Land, it's just filled with languages. You talk to a local person, and they will say this plant's called this, but other people call it that, and there they call it something else. They all know each other's languages.

SK: That's right.

RM: How did you get on with languages?

SK: I only learnt one or two languages really – the two biggest tribes. I did that because it was utterly impossible to learn all of their languages. I started with one language, and the languages of the two major tribes were really very simple. I couldn't speak the entire language, but I'd learned all the important words for food, river, fish, crocodiles, and things like that. They taught me a lot about crocodiles, what to do, where to go, how they come, and where they go, which helped me a lot. I swam in the rivers. I needed to know.

RM: When I talk to young people who haven't been out in the outback, they don't have any understanding of how dangerous crocodiles really are. What was your experience?

SK: They are very, very dangerous. When I was on my own travelling, which happened two or three times, I'd come to a river, and I'd walk along the river bank, until I found the bend in the river.

Below: *Crossing a river was incredibly dangerous in this part of Australia. There were no fords, no bridges and few boats, so you had to swim.*

Then I'd walk back to where I'd been, and back the other way, and then I'd walk back to where the middle of the river dipped – roughly the middle of the river, and I'd wait for the tide to turn. As the tide flowed out, the crocs would move up the river, and then they would wait for the tide to turn and come in. And, as the tide came in, the fish came in with the tide, and they would line up across the river, and feed themselves on fish that were coming in from the sea. At that stage, I would go back, far back, and then take a good look around, and swim the river, and pray to god there was nothing there. I swam a river once, and put my swag on the raft behind me. When I got out and I got up the bank, and under the shade of a big tree, there was a massive big crocodile, and he was lying there watching us. And I thought, *Oh my god*. All around him were scraps of meat, bits of legs and things – there must've been about two or three wallabies or, I don't know what it was actually. He had a bellyful.

RM: And they're incredibly fast, aren't they?

SK: That big fellow – I fired a shot over his head and he took off, and ran high up on his feet, his tail curved up over the top of his head, and he *went*. He must have gone about 15 feet through the air into the water with a hell of a big splash. They're fast and they're big.

RM: This method of crossing a river was a typical aboriginal thing, wasn't it? Because there were no roads.

Right: *Syd in December 1949.*

Above: *Ceremonies were held for many different purposes, including male initiation and commemoration of the dead.*

SK: No, there were no roads; they had to swim the rivers, and they used to swim in a group.

RM: Women and children, too?

SK: That's right. The men would swim behind them, in front of them and beside them with spears and all number of things attached. They were good – they can throw a spear from in the water, lift themselves up, throw it, and then back into the water – plonk.

RM: Every community that I've worked with in Arnhem Land can tell a story of people injured or killed by crocodiles.

SK: Yes, a lot. They're a very clever animal; they really are clever.

RM: And what would your advice be to anyone going into that part of Australia these days?

SK: Well, unless it's a question of life or death, don't swim in the river, don't attempt to swim in the river. Spend the time to cut a canoe out. On one river, the crocs were so bad, the aboriginals said to me, 'We're not going to swim. We've cut a tree down and we're cutting a canoe out of it on the track.'

RM: You had to cross lots of rivers, didn't you? You spent a lot of time on the Liverpool River, and that's home to some very big crocodiles.

SK: Yeah, there were small rivers and big rivers, and the crocs on the Liverpool River were very, very big. I went right up the Liverpool River, where it runs into the escarpment, which is absolutely incredible. From then on, there was no water.

RM: It's the Stone Country.

SK: Yes, the Stone Country – the aboriginals would not go into the Stone Country; they were absolutely scared stiff. Debil-debil, they called it – and everything else.

RM: They're quite superstitious people, aren't they?

SK: Extremely superstitious.

RM: One of the people you had very strong dealings with – your nemesis, if you like – was a spiritual leader, wasn't he?

SK: That's right, Mahrdei. He was a very old and clever man. And he treated me as an equal. He used to think I was something special. He said to me, 'Are you white man?' I said, 'Yes.' He said, 'Do you think you're a clever man?' I said, 'I'm clever for a white man and you're clever for a black man.' He looked at me, and said, 'Yeah, alright.' I said, 'What do you hear about white men?' 'They're no good,' he said. I said, 'Why do you say that?' He said that white men aren't honest; they tell too many lies. I said I'd argue with that! He said, 'Look: they tell you that you've got to go to some place they call a church, and then you've got to learn all about some person that lives up in the sky. You show me a man living in the sky – what's he sit on, a cloud? It's a heap of garbage. Nobody can live up in the clouds.'

RM: What do you make of their traditions?

SK: I respected them, I can say that much. I respected their traditions, and some of their traditions were very cruel. But I wouldn't ever intervene.

And perhaps that's the reason why Syd Kyle-Little was accepted into the heart of the aboriginal communities. While other white men and settlers worked with almost missionary zeal to impose order, strip the natives of their beliefs, their language and even their freedom, Syd acknowledged and accepted their differences. He took time to understand what they stood for, and how they lived, learning from them rather than trying to shape them to fit in with a white man's world. It is from Syd that much of our intimate knowledge of the aboriginal populations stems, and the beauty of their culture, mythology, language and heritage shines through in his book.

One of the greatest clues to the aboriginal identity and history can be found in their rock art, which harks back more than 40,000 years, making it one of the oldest of its kind in the world. I'll take you there next.

Right: *Stone Country; Syd got some of his trackers to pose with a cross.*

Rock Art

The rock art of the indigenous Australians is perhaps their greatest legacy and I find it absolutely fascinating. Across hundreds of thousands of square kilometres, rock art sites tell the story of their culture, history, spirituality, rituals and beliefs, creating what must be by far the world's largest art gallery. Art was not created for self-expression; instead it was a means of passing on ideas and values that had complex social significance, and represented the vibrant traditions and beliefs that are still maintained to this day.

When looking at rock art, it's important to realise the huge diversity that characterises Australia's indigenous people. There are some 250 languages spoken by the aboriginals and Torres Strait Islanders, and an equal number of tribes with different cultural values, spiritual beliefs and ways of subsisting. Before European settlement of Australia, there were around 600 different aboriginal nations,

Previous pages: *A picture of a black bream on a rock in the Kimberleys.*

Left: *Handprints are found in rock art all over the world.*

Above: *Eels tend to be associated with water in rock art. This example, which was around 10 metres long, was situated at an ancestral dwelling site near a river. As we arrived, JuJu Wilson told us to be careful because there could be snakes nearby and sure enough, ten paces later, there was a King Brown. Aboriginals often have a kind of telepathic awareness that you learn to trust.*

based on language groups. What united them was their affinity with the land, their belief in the 'Dreaming' – an English word used to describe stories about the creation of the land and the people – and their conviction that the natural world represents ancestral beings.

An aboriginal community does not own the land – rather it 'owns' them, for they have an inborn and unspoken obligation to the wellbeing of the land and the ancestral 'Dreaming' figures who created it. Every hill, every waterhole, every geographical feature is the result of the actions and interactions of creator beings as they travelled through the landscape. In some places these activities are more significant than in others.

In most stories of the Dreaming, ancestor spirits came to the earth in human form and as they moved through the land, they created the animals, plants, rocks and other natural forms. They also created the relationships between groups and individuals to the land, the animals and other people. Once the ancestor spirits had created the world, they changed into trees, stars, rocks, watering holes or other natural features. These remain the sacred places of aboriginal culture and each has its own special properties. Because the ancestors did not disappear at the end of the Dreaming, but remained in these sacred

sites, the Dreaming is never-ending, linking the past and the present, the people and the land. Time for them is not linear in the way it is for us; the past still exists just as much as the present. The landscape is not only a physical entity, but also has an intellectual content. Memories, myths, and ideas relating to the land are invisible but very vivid.

In many areas there are separate men's and women's stories. Knowledge of the law and of the Dreaming stories is acquired progressively as people proceed through life. Traditional ceremonies, such as initiation ceremonies, provide opportunities to pass on knowledge, as do the rock art sites. The stories and knowledge associated with many paintings often have a number of levels. Younger people and non-aboriginal people are told the first level, known as the 'public story'. Access to the 'full story' depends on an individual's progression through ceremonial life, their interest, and their willingness to take on the responsibilities that go with that knowledge.

Aboriginal artist Wenten Rubuntja said in the *Weekend Australian* magazine, that it's hard to find any art that is devoid of spiritual meaning: 'Doesn't matter what sort of painting we do in this country, it still belongs to the people, all the people. This is worship, work, culture. It's all Dreaming. There are two ways of painting. Both ways are important, because that's culture.'

The ancestral beings who created the land, seas, waterways, people, flora and fauna are known by different names depending on the local language.

The myths differ but they all have in common a serpent as the Creation Being – perhaps the oldest continuing religious belief in the world, dating back several thousands of years. The 'Rainbow Serpent' features in the Dreaming stories of many mainland aboriginal nations and is always associated with sources of water, such as billabongs, rivers, creeks and lagoons. The Rainbow Serpent is the protector of the land, its people, and the source of all life. However, it can also be a destructive force if it is not properly respected.

The most common version of the Rainbow Serpent story tells that in the Dreamtime, the world was flat, bare and cold. The Rainbow Serpent slept under the ground with all the animal tribes in her belly waiting to be born. When it was time, she arose, calling to the animals to come from their sleep. With the curves of her body, she pushed out the land, creating mountains and hills, and spilling water to create rivers and lakes. She was responsible for making the sun, the fire, and all of the colours.

The Gagudju people of the Kakadu region of northern Australia called the Rainbow Serpent Almudj. They believe that Almudj brings the wet season each year, which causes everything on the earth to grow and multiply, and she appears in the sky as a rainbow. Almudj must constantly be appeased, because she is also responsible for flooding, and will drown anyone who has broken laws. Almudj still lives in a pool under a waterfall in Kakadu.

The Jawoyn people, of the Katherine Gorge area in the Northern Territory, relate how the Rainbow Serpent slept under the ground until she awoke in the Dreaming and pushed her way to the surface. She then travelled the land, sleeping when she was tired, and leaving behind traces of her winding tracks and the imprint of her sleeping body. When she had travelled the earth, she returned and called to the frogs to come out, but they were very slow because their bellies were full of water. The Rainbow Serpent tickled their stomachs and when the frogs laughed, the water flowed out of their mouths and filled the tracks and hollows left by the Rainbow Serpent, creating the rivers and lakes. This woke all of the animals and plants, who then followed the Rainbow Serpent across the land.

To the peoples of the Torres Strait Islands, the Tagai, or warrior, features in most of their Dreamtime stories. As the Torres Strait Islanders are sea-faring people, the stories of the Tagai usually focus on stars.

ople drew from the Dreaming
laws and discipline. In aboriginal
edents, which means keeping the
nt way of retaining continuity with
vith the spirit world.

whole of Australia, even offshore islands,
holding their own stories. Tribe members
ity of 'owning' the story where it passed
vould be their job to maintain it – in other
y of doing this was through songs associated
is. They literally walked the storyline in religious
ceremonies, ar songs, and these lines became known as 'song'
or 'story' lines.

Song lines are an intricate series of song cycles that are associated with stories of the ancestral beings' passage across the land. Because of this, they became a useful means of navigating in territory that was too difficult to chart. By singing the songs in the appropriate sequence, indigenous peoples could navigate vast distances, even through the completely inhospitable deserts of the interior. The continent of Australia is snaked by song lines, some of which are just a few kilometres in length, and some of which traverse hundreds of kilometres through difficult terrain.

As they span the lands of several different language groups, different parts of the song are sung in those different languages. A whole song can only be fully understood by a person speaking all the relevant languages, but the caretaker or person walking the lines will know all of the words – or will be given them by the owners of that territory – and perform the necessary rituals en route, even if he does not understand exactly what he is saying or doing.

Following the song or story lines is not about re-enacting the past; instead, it involves retelling the story in a precise order, and undertaking the rituals that are part of the song or story. For example, there are certain ceremonies that will cause fruits to ripen on the trees and waterholes to remain full. These are very important, but it's impossible to get to the bottom of most of them because they are secret and sacred, and the aboriginals will not divulge information for fear of angering their ancestors. I once travelled a songline in the Central Desert with an old aboriginal woman and did the ceremonies associated with it. Not many white people have done that. I felt immensely privileged and wouldn't dream of repeating any of the stories I learned in this book, because that would be a betrayal of her trust.

Some anthropologists and scientists have noted that aboriginals possess an acute sensitivity to magnetic forces, and hypothesise that the song lines that meander across the continent system directly represent lines of energy that have now been charted. They link sacred place to sacred place, and could perhaps partly explain the aboriginals' uncanny ability to travel for months and even years across hostile land with nothing more than a song or story as a map.

There are 'maps' found in some of the rock art caves – not the kind of maps that you and I are used to, but obscure and beautiful maps that are nonetheless extremely accurate. They don't just reflect the attributes of the physical terrain, such as hills and waterholes, but in many cases they also depict events from the Dreamtime. Aboriginals couldn't even tell you all the things they've depicted because they'd be breaking their sacred laws to do so.

Some of them are very impressive. A rock art map can locate a waterhole of only a metre square in the whole of Australia. It's possible that each site provides information on how to continue on to the next sacred place, but the information is often so hidden in symbols, only caretakers or those gifted with knowledge could make it out. When you learn a little more about the native population, it's suddenly much easier to work out what is being said.

Author and aboriginal expert Pat Lowe (see page 118) confirms that aboriginal maps are like no other:

'The most graphic illustration I know of the difference between the perceptions of the desert of white and black Australians is in the maps we produce. In 1997, the Walmajarri Native Title claimants decided to present their claim to the Native Title Tribunal visually, in the form of a large painting. More than 50 artists

Above: *Some pictures are found high above ground in inaccessible-looking spots.*

collaborated to paint a map of their desert country over a canvas measuring eight metres by ten metres, each artist taking responsibility for representing the right area for his or her family group. Compare this extraordinary cooperative work with an Ordnance Survey map of the desert, and you will see what it means to belong.'

Some journeys undertaken by aboriginals in the old days were staggering in their length. They would commonly take two or three months to walk the whole journey around the sacred sites on the line where it crossed their land; longer lines could sometimes take two years or more. Traditionally they travelled with just spears and firesticks to catch and cook their food along the way. Today they go by car, with water and supplies on board, but their caretaking responsibilities can still take them away from home for long periods. These journeys

through the bush are an admirable feat, even using modern methods of survival. I travelled with JuJu Wilson, a well-known contemporary aboriginal artist, to one sacred place in the Kimberleys. It was a two-hour trip by car but she told us that her grandfather used to walk the same route, a trip that would take him eight weeks. The devotion and sense of obligation felt by these men is unbelievable.

The sacred sites along the song line routes were almost always decorated with rock art. Some sites tell the story of who had passed through the land, including natives and white settlers; others pass on laws, have ceremonial importance, represent burial sites and important places of initiation; all provide refuges from the ferocity of the natural environment, and they usually have a water source nearby.

In northern Australia there are numerous sandstone rock shelters where the art is particularly prolific. Many of these have been used for camping and their floors are layered with charcoal and ash from camp fires, the remains of food such as shells and animal bones, stone tools and, very often, pieces of ochre. Ochre comes from soft varieties of iron oxide minerals and is used to create red and yellow colours. Glues are made of the gum from trees or from animal fluids such as eyeball juice. You see where the aboriginals mixed their paint, where they sharpened their spears, where they cooked a meal, and perhaps lay down to rest.

Every cave or rock shelter tells a story through its art, and through the care taken to protect its surroundings. Many of them can't be visited by non-aboriginals, because they are too sacred and too secret. Some are close to burial sites of important elders and spiritual leaders; others tell stories that the aboriginals simply wish to keep to themselves. The crew and I were taken to some secret places but not allowed to film there.

As soon as we arrived at the site JuJu took us to, outside Kununurra in the Kimberleys, she sat on the ground under a tree while the crew began unloading their equipment. I watched her as she sat there, listening intently, and looking towards the rocks. Then she began to shout out in her local

Above: *JuJu Wilson calling to her ancestors to tell them that we were there and explain why we were visiting the site. Aboriginals believe that their ancestors continue to live but in a different dimension to us.*

Previous pages: *JuJu sitting in a well-worn rock shelter. She was very comfortable and at peace there.*

Following pages: *A view of the Kimberley coast from the air.*

language, greeting her ancestors. Her words were something like: 'Hello, it's me. I've brought some strangers today to look at the art.' To her, the ancestors were still vibrantly alive there, watching and judging the actions of the living. It was very touching to witness and helped to make sense of the art we were about to view as well.

JuJu explained to us that in every generation the old rock paintings must be refreshed or they will fade away – but not just anyone can do the refreshing. You need to have the requisite knowledge, and to know the correct stories. Certain rituals are required, and only those invested with the authority to do so may paint or repaint here, to maintain the health of the site and the creator being, who is believed to dwell within its image in the rock.

She told us that anyone who did not have custodianship of the sacred site could not repaint or refresh the art without running the risk of falling ill. We heard the story of a painting that had been refreshed by someone who didn't know the correct rituals and ceremonies, and everyone there died. JuJu herself says she asks permission of the ancestors before refreshing any paintings.

This is a strong belief, and it is one reason why many rock art paintings are no longer maintained to the same degree as they were in the past. Aboriginal people no longer live in rock shelters and there are fewer people with the necessary knowledge to allow them to paint at certain sites. It used to be that the skills and stories were passed down from generation to generation. Aboriginal artist Billy Lukanawi says he was shown the proper painting style by his father and uncle: 'I've got to draw that same one, that same drawing: kangaroo, turtle, crocodile, rainbow [snake], quiet snake, file snake. I've got to draw the same way my father, my uncle [drew]; I've got to do red, yellow, and white … the same way.'

With the move into towns, and as people who have custodianship of sites die without passing on their knowledge, old sites are no longer refreshed and techniques are lost. But in spite of this, rock art remains relevant: it depicts objects still used, animals still hunted, and activities people still do today.

The rock art of the Australian aboriginals represents the longest continuously practised series of artistic traditions anywhere in the world, and it is almost impossible to date. In fact, attempting to date it often raises more questions than it answers. The widely accepted view is that it's at least 60,000 years old, but a relatively new technique called thermoluminescence dating found a piece of art that was at least 75,000 years old. To put this into perspective, that's almost ten times older than the Egyptian pyramids. And some archaeologists claim to have found tools at the sites which date another 100,000 years back. Evidence of charcoal remains near Canberra suggests that firestick farming (or intentional burning of the bush) was used there between 80,000 and 100,000 years ago.

There is a recent theory that Australian aboriginals might have been the first human beings on the planet, and not central Africans as is more usually believed. According to this theory, people migrated from Australia to the rest of the world so some of their art may represent the very earliest prehistoric cave paintings. I don't believe it though – all the DNA evidence points to the first humans coming from Africa.

The process of dating the art is often complicated by the fact that many works have been painted over – and not always with the same images. Updating, telling new stories, and passing on new wisdom, as told by the ancestral spirits, often meant older works were replaced, and made their dating impossible. In some cases it is possible to relate certain styles and types of subject matter to key dates, but even contemporary artists use traditional methods, pigments and images so that doesn't help. And as we've said, types and styles of rock art vary enormously across the continent and between aboriginal groups.

In western Arnhem Land, archaeologists recognise three periods: Pre-Estuarine (drier climate, extinct animals like thylacine), Estuarine (rising sea levels, marine fauna like barramundi and salt-water crocodiles, Rainbow Serpent), and Freshwater (freshwater fauna like magpie geese, goose feather adornment). Images of freshwater fauna showing internal anatomy (the X-ray style – see page 104) only appeared in the last 3,000 years. Pictures recording contact with Europeans (showing boats and guns) can only be a few hundred years old. You can also hazard a guess at dates through

the weaponry depicted: boomerangs are replaced by composite spears and broad spear-throwers, which are then replaced by long spear-throwers.

In the Kimberley region, aboriginals claim that the very oldest pictures were made by birds that pecked the rocks until their beaks bled and then painted the images with their tail feathers. This art form was first recorded by Joseph Bradshaw in 1891, when he was lost on a Kimberley expedition in the north-west of Australia and came across a wall of colourful paintings. He described them in the 'Transactions' of the Royal Geographical Society of Victoria in 1892:

'We saw numerous caves and recesses in the rocks, the walls of which were adorned with native drawings coloured in red, black, brown, yellow, white and a pale blue. Some of the human figures were life size, the bodies and limbs were attenuated and represented as having numerous tassel-shaped adornments appended to their hair, neck, waist, arms and legs; but the most remarkable fact in connection with these drawings is that whenever a profile face is shown the features are of a most pronounced aquiline type, quite different from the natives we encountered. Indeed, looking at some of the groups one might think himself viewing the painted walls of an Egyptian temple. These sketches seemed to be a great age.'

Since then tens of thousands more sites have been found in the Kimberley region with similar paintings, now known as Bradshaw art. Bradshaw art depicts human-like, predominantly genderless figures, which are characterised by extensive and elaborate head-dresses, often with knotted trails, and elaborate body ornamentation. When in the presence of this art, you are requested to be very quiet and reverent. Some figures appear in hunting scenes, others in festive dances with

Previous pages: *Rock art on the coast of the Kimberleys showing a dug-out canoe and visitors from another country smoking pipes. They were probably from the Torres Straits and came over to trade with local aboriginals.*

Right: *Bradshaw figures. You can see why people might think they are African dancers.*

a great deal of movement; some appear to be passing objects from one to the other in a kind of ceremony; still others appear to be threatening, as if warning the viewer of some magical or mysterious danger.

In 1955, Dr Andreas Lommel studied the Unambal tribe of aboriginals living in north-west Australia, and announced that in his opinion the rock art referred to as Bradshaw art might well predate the present Australian aboriginals. This art is of such antiquity that no pigment remains on the rock surface, so it is impossible to use carbon dating technology, but a fossilised wasp's nest covering one of the paintings has been dated as at least 17,000 years old. The composition of the original paints cannot be determined, and whatever pigments were used have been locked into the rock itself as shades of mulberry red, and have become impervious to the elements. Blank spaces indicate that many other colours may have been used, as Joseph Bradshaw obviously saw when he came across them.

The art is very different from that created by the aboriginals who were living in the area at the time of European colonisation, known as Wandjinas. Although Wandjina paintings also depict the human form, their figures are simply replicated over and over, they lack fine detail in line construction, and they don't use hieroglyphic-style symbols. The diversity, refinement, and replication of symbols in Bradshaw art seems reminiscent of a culture that wanted to use art for a purpose other than ceremony or religion.

Learning to paint on a cave wall is very difficult, and the Bradshaw artists don't show the signs of evolution from a culture that grew from painted silhouettes of hands to a culture that painted extremely detailed pictures. On the contrary, the Bradshaw paintings appear in their most

Left, top and bottom: *Bradshaw art, with its beautiful, mysterious figures. We'll never know who painted them and when.*

advanced style, continue for perhaps 20,000 years, and then vanish.

Several experts have remarked that Bradshaw figures are very reminiscent of the art created by the nomadic tribes that still occupy Africa and were known to wander through Asia way back in the past. There is no other art like the Bradshaws anywhere in Australia; its unique style and depiction of body adornment is not characteristic of aboriginal people and the facial features that Bradshaw described were not aboriginal ones. Could it be that the paintings were created by people from Africa, who possibly arrived in the past and then departed again? This is an interesting theory. I'm particularly intrigued by it, because near to many of these Bradshaw sites there are baobab trees (known locally as 'boab'). These trees are indigenous to Africa, and analysis has found that the

Below and right: *The boab tree is native to Africa. I've used it a lot there and found many uses for it: you can make fire with the wood, eat the leaves, or make a vitamin-C-rich drink from the fruit inside the nuts. But were boabs brought to Australia by early travellers from Africa?*

species around the art sites is, in fact, the same genetic strain as the baobab in Madagascar, which lies off the south-east coast of Africa.

Certainly it's possible that the seeds from those trees floated across the ocean and established themselves on the northern coast of Australia. This is a theory that Pat Lowe subscribes to. In her book *The Boab Tree* (1998) she writes:

'Although such a means of dispersal may sound unlikely, particularly in view of prevailing currents and winds which have been found to carry Indonesian seeds west rather than east, Baobab seeds would not be the only ones known to have drifted east across the Indian Ocean. The Coco de Mer palm of the Seychelles Islands is one plant whose seeds, carried in huge buoyant pods, have been found washed up on the shores of Western Australia. An even more unlikely arrival from Madagascar discovered on the coast of Western Australia is an enormous egg from the now extinct Elephant Bird (Aepyornis sp.).'

But perhaps it's possible that the seeds were brought to Australia by settlers or explorers, migrants from Madagascar itself, and used as survival rations? If the pod of the baobab seed isn't cracked, the fruit inside can last for years, and it is highly nutritious – so nutritious that the juice from a single fruit has more than five times the vitamin C of an orange. Pat Lowe explains how the seeds may have been used and, indeed, can still be used today:

'The Boab provided people with food in several forms, of which the best known is found within the pod or nut. The ripe nut is filled with a dry, brittle, powdery white pith, the texture of Styrofoam, in which the seeds are embedded. The pith, though mouth-drying and flavourless at first bite, contains vitamin C and tastes acidic when chewed. People eat it as it comes out of the shell, or crush it up with water and drink the wet pulp like a cordial. In earlier times they used to sweeten the liquid with the honey of native bees, more recently with sugar. Connoisseurs of Boab nuts tell me that the contents vary considerably in sweetness of taste.'

My personal experience is that it tastes like a delicious light lemonade, tart but hugely thirst-quenching. It makes sense that these seeds would be a useful, if not essential ration for travellers from afar, and to my mind, it feeds the theory that they may not have made their way here by sea but were brought by these early travellers.

Something else that makes me curious about the baobab trees found near Bradshaw art sites is the fact that from the air, they look as though they have been planted. Their pattern distribution is entirely different to that of the African baobabs which have grown naturally.

Could the Bradshaws be African? Until recently local aboriginals didn't claim them as their own, but in recent years, as it has become possible for them to claim land rights over sacred sites, their views have changed. It seems to me that this is a mystery that might never be solved.

Not all rock art is as contentious as Bradshaw art. Most other examples can be dated and grouped according to style, age and theme. Mimi art, for example, is believed to be the first rock art painted by the aboriginals. The Warradjan Aboriginal Cultural Centre in Kakadu, claims: 'Mimi spirits were the first of the Creation Ancestors to paint on rock. They taught some Aboriginal people how to paint and other Aboriginal people learned by copying Mimi art. At the end of their journeys, some Creation Ancestors put themselves on rock walls as paintings and became *djang* (Dreaming places). Some of these paintings are *andjamun* (sacred and dangerous) and can be seen only by senior men or women; others can be seen by all people.'

Mimi drawings, usually in red ochre, show elegant, graceful stick-like human figures in action – fighting, running, dancing, leaping and hunting. The Mimi were said to live in the nooks and crannies of the rocky landscape, coming out at night. They are so thin and frail that they can emerge from their hiding places only when there is no wind, otherwise they would be blown away.

The Worrorra, Wunambal, and Ngarinyin people of north-western and central Kimberley believe that the Wandjina are the Creation Beings of the Dreaming, and that they made their world and all that it contains. Wandjina paintings are found in many rock art sites in caves and rock shelters throughout the Kimberley region.

Wandjina are usually painted as either full-length or head-and-shoulder figures, who can be standing or lying horizontally. Their large mouthless faces feature enormous black eyes flanking a beak-like nose. The head is

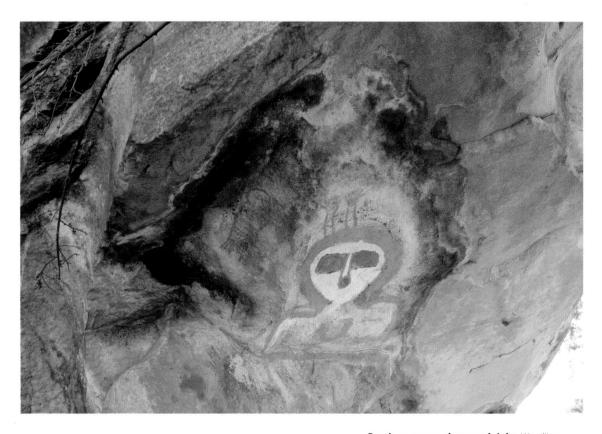

usually surrounded by a band with outward radiating lines. Elaborate headdresses represent both the hair of the Wandjinas and clouds. Long lines coming out from the hair are the feathers that Wandjinas wore, and the lightning, which they control.

Wandjina ceremonies to ensure the timely beginning of the monsoon wet season and bring sufficient rainfall are held during December and January, following which the rains usually begin. In paintings, Wandjina spirits were never given mouths, because the aboriginals believed that everything would be flooded and drowned. If the Wandjina are offended, they take their revenge by calling up lightning to strike the offender dead, or calling upon the rain to flood the land and drown the people, or a cyclone with its winds to devastate the country. These are the powers which the Wandjinas could supposedly use.

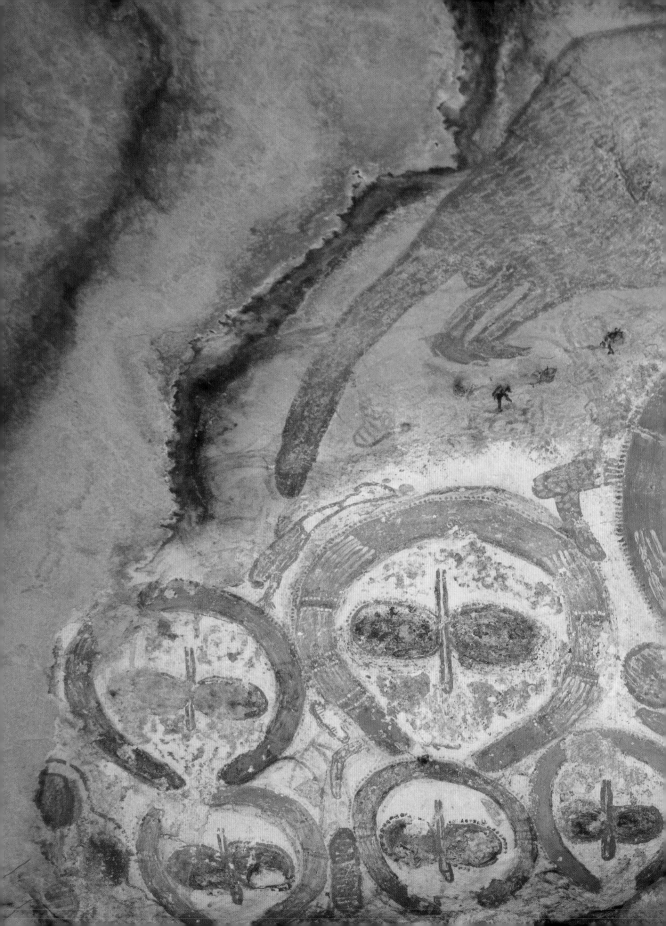

Wandjina images don't only appear in paintings, but have for many millennia been carved on bark 'coolamons', a type of carrier which was used for food gathering and as cradles for newborn babes; on ceremonial boomerangs and shields; and on a myriad of other symbolic artefacts.

Some types of rock art record mythological stories, sorcery, fertility and death rituals, while others depict the hunt. It was believed that drawing a particular animal would stimulate the species to propagate and that the ritual act of painting or touching these depictions would release sacred energy or power. The rock art in Kakadu, for example, depicts hunting (animals were often painted to ensure a successful hunt by placing people in touch with the spirit of the animal); religious significance (at some sites paintings depict aspects of particular ceremonies); stories and learning (associated with the Creation Ancestors, who gave shape to the world); and sorcery and magic (in which paintings could be used to manipulate events and influence people's lives).

In Arnhem Land and Kakadu, a style of X-ray rock art is found in which the skeletons and viscera of the animals and humans portrayed are drawn inside the outline, as if by cross section. This tradition is believed to have developed about 2000 BC, and it continues today in contemporary art. X-ray art includes sacred images of ancestral supernatural beings as well as secular works depicting fish and animals that were important food sources. In many instances, the paintings show fish and game species from the local area, and provide vital information on how to use flora and fauna.

Previous pages: *Wandjina figures with a kangaroo. The animals don't have mouths either.*

Right: *Wandjina crocodiles. This painting is on a rock that is shaped like the head of a crocodile (see the lower picture on page 106).*

Above and left: *According to JuJu Wilson, these paintings were refreshed by people who did not have the right to do so and they all fell ill and died.*

First of all, a silhouette of the figure was painted, often in white, and then the internal details were added in red or yellow. For red, yellow, and white paints, artists use natural ochre pigments mined from mineral deposits, while black is derived from charcoal. Early X-ray images depict the backbone, ribs, and internal organs of humans and animals. Later examples also include features such as muscle groups, body fat, optic nerves, and breast milk in women. Some works created after European contact even show rifles with the bullets visible inside them. As historical documents, these paintings are invaluable.

One of the best known X-ray painting sites is at Ubirr, in the north-east of Kakadu, which served as a camping place during the annual wet season. Here, the artists painted mostly fish like barramundi, but also turtles, birds and reptiles. There is even a painting of a European, with his hands in his pockets. Many paintings are less than 1,500 years old, but there is an image of the Rainbow Serpent on a cliff wall above what was probably an occupation site that could go back as far as 23,000 years. (Aboriginals argue that they and their ancestors have been occupying the land forever, and therefore it cannot be 'dated'.)

Similar X-ray paintings are found throughout the region, including the site of Injaluk near the community of Gunbalanya (also called Oenpelli), whose contemporary aboriginal artists continue to create works in the X-ray tradition.

One of the richest of these areas is at what is now Kakadu National Park, the traditional lands of the Gagudju people, in the Top End, just west of Arnhem Land. There are many sites that are not open to visitors, like the cave with the Blue Paintings, of fairly recent origin; these are known as 'Reckitts Blue', because an agent to clean clothes was used as well as traditional ochres. This site is now closed to visitors at the request of the traditional owners because there is a burial cave nearby but there are superb examples of rock art in the galleries of Nourlangie Rock and Ubirr, where visitors can view them easily while the paintings are protected from vandals – sadly still a problem here as in other parts of the world. Many ancient rock sites have been devastated by graffiti, and the so-called 'advance' of civilisation. Recently, it was revealed that almost 5,000 aboriginal petroglyphs (images created by removing part of a rock surface by incising, pecking, carving, and abrading) have been destroyed on the Burrup peninsula through the exploitation of oil and gas reserves.

'Nourlangie' is the English name for the area traditionally known as Nawurlandja. The upper part and the lower areas of Nourlangie Rock are respectfully known as Burrungguy and Anbangbang. According to the traditional Creation story, mythical short-eared rock wallaby Creation Ancestors travelled past Nourlangie Rock, across the Anbangbang billabong, and went up into the rocks at Nawurlandja. There they cut two crevices in the rock, still visible today. Rock wallabies can often be seen in the early morning and late afternoon. Burrungguy or Nourlangie Rock's main art site is the Anbangbang, with beautiful examples of X-ray art, like the painting of Namondjok and Namarrgon, the Lightning Man.

Stencil art is another common form of aboriginal art, and its main function is as a record of people's presence and association with a site. I saw many examples of hand- and footprints sprayed in ochre. It's important to remember that these rock art sites were very personal – they told a story of the people who had been and gone, and the link these people had with the land around them. So you might find handprints that have been there for thousands of years alongside much newer ones, as well as images of the wildlife in the area, what you might eat, where you'd find water, and which spiritual ancestors were indigenous to the site. There would be symbols telling you it's a burial site, and something that tells you the nature of the person or people who were buried there. It's very intimate. There would be handprints and footprints of children and old men and women. These were the way that the natives left their mark, the way they connected with the rocks, who held their ancestors, the way they told their stories in a time before there was any written word.

One old man I talked to in Arnhem Land remembered being carried as a child on his father's shoulders as his father climbed up a log leaning against a rock wall. His father then held his hand against the rock and sprayed it

Above: *Was this the footprint of a European explorer arriving in the Kimberleys? Whoever they were, they were obviously wearing shoes.*

with red ochre, leaving a stencil he could still recognise many years later. He also showed me his grandmother's handprint from when she was five. I was curious to find out how they sprayed the paint, and was told that they mixed water, blood or spittle with ochre and other rock pigments and took a mouthful of the mixture then spat it in a fine spray directly onto the rock, to produce an effect similar to modern spray paint. It is a tradition that still, although dying out, continues to some extent this day.

Dot painting is a technique that is still widely used. Dot paintings tell stories that were traditionally drawn in the sand or on the rock face to teach the culture and impart the traditional ways of the aboriginal people to their young. They represent the aboriginal's 'written word', if you like, and they tell about the time of the Dreaming, when the ancestors roamed the countryside, shaping it into what we now see.

As the name suggests, these paintings consist of thousands of 'dots' and, done the traditional way, it can take the artist many days of dedicated concentration just to fill in the background. Their tools were originally feathers, sticks, echidna quills or spikes, and stones dipped into natural pigments.

The traditional aboriginal dot paintings usually represent a story, generally regarding hunting or food gathering. They are sources of information about the local area, the rock art site itself, the spiritual associations, and the rituals that must be performed by the caretakers. They are everything from local map, story and song, to rulebook, local history and spiritual guide. Most importantly, however, they tell the stories of the Dreaming, and how they came to be.

When you look a little closer, what seems at first to be a series of interconnected and in some cases unrelated images are in fact a series of symbols or 'icons' in the paintings. These symbols, when explained, give a whole new meaning to the work. There are symbols for rain, ants, paths, tracks, spear throwers, snakes, rivers, footprints, boomerangs, hills and campsites. This information would have been invaluable to any native who came upon them, and provide us, today, with a fascinating insight into the way the aboriginals have lived their lives across the millennia. I can't tell you what a profound experience it is to see the stories of so many hundreds of generations of natives.

In other areas, there are still more techniques and styles used; for example, in Queensland, simple figurative painted or engraved silhouettes can be found. In Central Australia, the Kimberleys, Tasmania and areas of Victoria, it's common to find engraved geometric figures, such as circles, concentric circles, arcs, animal tracks and dots.

Left: *Handprints leave a unique, personal record of past generations.*

Rock art sites proliferate around the country. Captain Arthur Phillip, first Governor of New South Wales, wrote in 1788 of a probable 2,000 rock engraving sites on the local sandstone outcroppings, in the neighbourhood of Botany Bay and Port Jackson: 'The figures of animals, of shields, and weapons, and even of men, have been seen carved upon the rocks, roughly indeed, but sufficiently well to ascertain very fully what was the object intended. Fish were often represented, and in one place the form of a large lizard was sketched out with tolerable accuracy. On the top of one of the hills, the figure of a man in the attitude usually assumed by them when they begin to dance, was executed in a still superior style.'

Sydney rock art has its own peculiar symbolism, not found elsewhere in Australia, with beautiful carved animals and humans. Many thousands of such engravings are known to exist in the Sydney region, although the locations of most are not publicised to prevent damage by vandals, and to retain their sanctity, as they are still regarded as sacred sites by aboriginals. The Sydney engravings are of a style known as 'simple figurative', which conventional archaeological thinking dates to the last 5,000 years. It is likely that some of the freshest engravings represent the later part of that time range, whilst the most worn represent the earliest part. However, the situation is complicated by the fact that the engravings were sometimes 're-grooved' during ceremonies. It has been claimed that some engravings appear to show Thylacines and other mammals, which have been extinct in the Sydney region for many thousands of years – and so are presumably that old.

Wherever you go in the country, the deep and vibrant history of the aboriginals, their intrinsic beliefs, and their unique way of translating their stories and their spirituality into art are all reasons why today's aboriginal artists carry on many of the same traditions.

Aboriginal artists continue to paint on bark, paper and other materials. In recent years printing traditional designs onto fabric has become a popular art form, particularly among women. While aboriginal painting traditions are many thousands of years old, it was not until the 1970s that indigenous artists began to receive widespread recognition in the West. Perhaps the most famous group of that era was the Australian Western Desert artists of Papunya Tula.

The Papunya Tula artists are mainly known for their use of the 'dot' style of painting, and are now considered one of the most widely recognised schools of aboriginal painting. There are, however, many others. Bark paintings, weavings, sculptures, headdresses (particularly from the Torres Strait Islanders) and even painted hollow log coffins by the artists of Ramingining in Arnhem Land are now found in national collections, and purchased by people around the world.

Once a local schoolteacher, Geoffrey Bardon (1940–2003), introduced modern paints and canvas to his community, many locals began adapting their styles to take advantage of these new, Western mediums. The result was a flourishing art movement throughout the Western Desert that encouraged both individuals and whole communities to tell their stories and lay down their symbolic icons onto canvas.

One of the best known artists was Albert Namatjira (d. 1959), who became internationally renowned for his figurative landscapes. He was, in fact, the first aboriginal painter to receive recognition for his art outside Australia. His landscape paintings usually depicted areas he had known throughout his life in the tribal land of Western Aranda, central Australia, and his work went on to inspire the Hermannsburg School of landscape painting.

In the late 1980s and early 1990s, the work of Emily Kngwarreye became very popular. She had been involved in craftwork for most of her life, and it was only in her eighties that she was recognised as a painter. From the Utopia community north-east of Alice Springs, Kngwarreye painted for only a few years near the end of her life. Her styles, which changed every year, were a mixture of traditional aboriginal and contemporary Australian. Her rise in popularity prefigured that of many indigenous artists from central, northern and Western Australia, such as Kngwarreye's niece Kathleen Petyarre, Minnie Pwerle, Dorothy Napangardi, Jeannie Petyarre (Pitjara) and dozens of others, all of whose works have become highly sought after.

Rock art subjects and style have been transmuted into a portable form that can be bought and displayed around the world. Artists work on canvas

now and, while they still use earth pigments, instead of using tree gum to hold the pigments together, they use PVA wood glue and water, which is very effective. There are some truly beautiful – stunning – works of art using old themes and images, for example, animals, birds, the crocodile, wallabies.

However, I worry that as the work has become more commercialised, artists are being swayed from traditional ways by flash gallery owners, who say things like: 'Do more of this style/colour/size of canvas because it will look good on the wall of a New York loft apartment.' Traditional stories can only be cheapened by commissions to match interior décor, but it's true that in any style of art, there are good and bad artists. There are those who paint to impart deep meanings and those who are happy to decorate the lids of biscuit tins, so long as it pays enough.

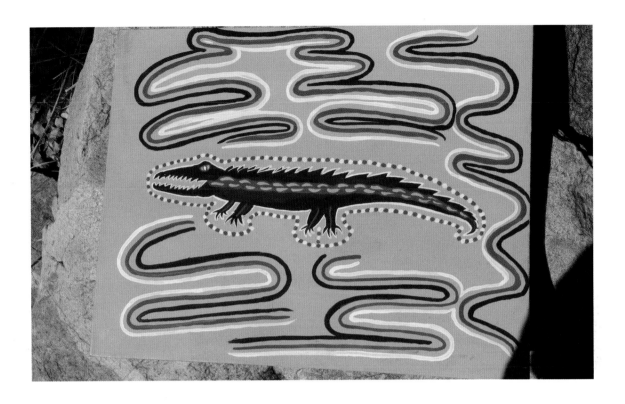

There is one aboriginal artist who remains close to my heart. JuJu Wilson, who, as I described earlier, did me the great honour of taking me to her sacred ancestral site in the Kimberleys, showed me her working methods and even encouraged me to do my own 'aboriginal-style' painting, which you can see on page 115.

JuJu is unique. She's a mother of six, a prolific painter, tour guide, cultural advisor; she's incredibly knowledgeable about bush tucker and bush medicine, and she is the author of many booklets on these subjects. She appears on TV, makes didgeridoos and plays them, is an authority on rock art and sacred sites, and speaks five dialects fluently.

JuJu was born in Mantinea Flats in East Kimberley. Her aboriginal name is Burriwee, but everyone just calls her JuJu. She used to watch her grandfather painting, and she started copying him, at first just doing goannas, snakes and turtles. Like many aboriginals, she believes that painting keeps their culture alive. She is aghast at the devastation being caused to the Australian landscape and the wildlife that is being destroyed by pollution and bushfires. She wonders if the next generation will ever see a wallaby, a barramundi or a kangaroo, and that is one reason why she strives to keep them 'alive' in her work.

JuJu's paintings and artefacts are now collected worldwide. She likes to paint animals and favours the landscapes around Kununurra to Purnululu (Bungle Bungles). She also carves and, while we were filming, she sat and carved a ground pigeon out of a boab shell, painting its features delicately in red ochre.

Left: *Pat Lowe is a lovely lady, who offers a fascinating insight into aspects of aboriginal life that few Westerners have been privy to. Her experience probably won't be repeated because the old knowledge is rapidly being lost.*

Another faithful defender of aboriginal identity is Pat Lowe, who I met on my travels. Pat was born in England and migrated to Australia in 1972. After giving up teaching, she studied psychology and started working in prisons. It was in Fremantle Prison near Broome that she met aboriginal artist Jimmy Pike, a convicted murderer who had grown up in the Great Sandy Desert. In 1986 when he was released from prison, Lowe joined him at his camp in the sandhills. The pair spent the next three years in the desert, hunting and exploring Pike's ancestral country. While Pike painted, Lowe wrote her first book, based on her experiences with Pike, who supplied many of its illustrations.

Pat has travelled in the Great Sandy Desert, dug waterholes, taken part in many hunts, and learned how to track. She has an amazing number of anecdotes, often humorous, which truly bring the aboriginals to life. Her experiences with Jimmy gave her enormous insight into the traditions behind aboriginal art, and as she sat alongside him, watching him work, and often living the life of the ancestors, she was able to understand the depth of spirit that goes into the art, and how the simplicity of the figures denotes something much more profound.

Like JuJu, Pat is a staunch defender of aboriginal traditions and identity, and her insights into their art are based on personal experience, and a deep love of the people and the countryside. Commenting on the current Land Rights debate, she says: 'There's no way you can have monetary compensation for the loss of people's culture and heritage. That's what they lose when they lose their land. People say, what about the pastoralists? But to quote Mick Dodson [an indigenous Australian leader], they're renters. It drives me mad when you hear over and over again that 70 per cent of Australia is under native title claim. What I want to know is why it isn't 100 per cent?'

It's a good question. This is a land that resonates with the past, and has been carefully maintained and nurtured across thousands and thousands of years, by people who believe they are the land itself, and who believe that the land gives them their identities and their reason for living. Rock art is only one example of a vital past that has imbued Australia with so many of her magical, mystical qualities, and these often simple drawings tell a story, sing a song, re-enact a ceremony, and bring alive a spirituality and oneness

Above: *JuJu with some little gremlin-like creatures depicted in the Kimberleys.*

that would be hard to match. What is the future for rock art? This fading art is testament to a culture that once proliferated and to lots of animal species that may become extinct over the coming decades. Rock art is a litmus of the health of Australia's cultural heritage. It's the front line.

In the Land of the Bush Tucker Man

Bush Two

One of my aims when I went 'walkabout' in Australia was to visit parts of the continent I'd never been to before. I was especially intrigued by the north-eastern state of Queensland, a land criss-crossed by explorers over the generations, and still home to a number of aboriginal tribes. The landscapes encompass humid, lush tropical rainforest, near-impassable rocky mountains and dense scrubland, and some of the most inhospitable terrain of the Australian outback. Even with modern transportation methods, this land is intimidating and difficult to negotiate; in some places, it is impossible to see more than 10 feet in front of you, and it can take hours to clear landing space for a helicopter. I wanted to experience this challenging wilderness firsthand, and to find the site of one of the most celebrated survival legends of Australia – the crash of a plane called 'Little Eva' in 1942, from which one man managed to achieve the impossible and survive the elements and the barren landscape for almost five months.

Left: *A forked twig is a handy tool for suspending your billycan over a fire.*

We set out from the east of Queensland, a state dominated by coastline. Even today, most settlement is concentrated on a narrow coastal strip characterised by lush rainforests and, just offshore, the Great Barrier Reef. This is the area where Captain Cook moored the *Endeavour* for repairs (see pages 25–27). Just a few miles further south, the Daintree River opens into a giant sandbar that shifts with each changing tide, causing problems for ship captains who want to enter the river. It winds inland through mangrove swamps where the water remains salty and then gradually turns fresh as it progresses through the Daintree Rainforest.

Just inland from here is the Great Dividing Range, which consists of a complex of mountain ranges, plateaus, upland areas and escarpments with an ancient and complex geological history. The crest of the range is defined by the watershed or boundary between the drainage basins of the rivers that flow directly eastward into the Pacific Ocean, and those which drain into the Murray-Darling River system towards the west. In the north, the rivers on the west side of the range flow towards the Gulf of Carpentaria.

These ranges were originally home to Australian aboriginal tribes, such as the Kulin. Evidence remains of their occupation in some places, with decorated caves, campsites and trails they used to travel between the coastal and inland regions. Europeans began to settle in the area from 1788, but they found the mountains an obstacle to exploration. Although not high, parts of the Great Dividing Range are incredibly rugged.

To the west of the range are the tablelands, fertile areas of flat agricultural land that lead to the barren outback, which continues into the Northern Territory. In the far northern Gulf Country (where Little Eva crashed) and Cape York Peninsula, there are huge empty regions cut by a multitude of dry riverbeds, which become overflowing rivers and staggeringly beautiful, rushing waterfalls in the wet season.

There are basically two seasons in Northern Queensland and the coastal regions: 'hot and wet' in summer and 'cool and dry' in winter. November to April or May is the wetter, hotter half of the year, while the 'wet season', particularly affecting the northern coastal areas takes place from January to March. This is also the season for tropical cyclones, which can devastate communities, causing widespread gales and flooding. The humidity caused by the heat and rain provides a breeding ground for countless insects and other plant and animal life, including snakes, which can make traversing the country even more difficult. Crocodiles move further inland in the wet season, into bogs created by the overflowing rivers and estuaries, and plant life grows at a spectacular rate, making dense scrub and rainforest impenetrable.

The Kuku Yalariji aborigines, who live in coastal Queensland, particularly in the Daintree Rainforest, distinguish five seasons, based on the typical weather patterns of that period. Kambar is the proper wet season, and runs from late December to March; Kabakababa is the winter rain season from April to May, and Buluriji is the cold season, from June to September. Wungariji is the hot season, from October to November, while the end of November to the middle of December marks Jarramali, or the 'stormy season', when weather conditions can be extreme.

In the Gulf Country the Yanyuwa aborigines have different distinctions. January and February is the Wunthurru, or early storm period; March to June is Lhabayi, or the proper wet season, with heavy rainfall; June and July is Rra-mardu, or the dry season, with sunny cloudless days and cool evenings, sometimes with heavy dews and fogs; August and September is Ngardaru, the hot weather time, with hot strong winds and dust storms, and extremely arid conditions; while October to December marks Na-yinarramba, which is hot and humid.

So even within the same state, the weather can change dramatically from month to month, and the conditions vary across the different types of terrain. Anyone wishing to travel across northern Queensland from east to west must be prepared for sudden and dramatic changes in temperature, geography, animal and plant life, and, of course, access to water sources. In the build-up season, before the heavy rains, many animals – in particular snakes – can behave oddly and aggressively, perhaps because they are sensitive to the barometric changes. Toxic snakes that usually show little interest in humans suddenly become angry and temperamental as the ground heats up. Only the taipan, found in north Australia, is aggressive, though. The King Brown, one of the world's most poisonous snakes, will often follow humans, using its strong sense of smell to track them. This snake is best avoided at all times of the year, although certain aboriginal tribes used to eat the flesh. I invited

Australia's famous 'Bush Tucker Man', Les Hiddins, to accompany me on my journey across Queensland, sharing with me his knowledge of the land and the bush food to be found there. No Australian is better known to survival enthusiasts than Les. He is almost single-handedly responsible for creating a renaissance of interest in bush tucker, opening up parts of Australia to the masses through his television programmes and many books. We had more in common than I dared hope, and straight away we realised that we shared a methodology and a love of the vast unknown of the Australian continent. We were determined to put our own skills to the test, and also work out how the Little Eva survivors and other early explorers managed to survive so many years ago.

Les spent his childhood in Cairns and Brisbane, on the coast of Queensland. He joined the Australian army in 1966 as a private infantry soldier, and took two tours of Vietnam between 1966 and 1969. In 1975 he led the 'Pudding Pan Hill Expedition' in search of the explorer Edmund Kennedy's death site on the Cape York Peninsula (see page 34), and in 1977 began private and self-funded research into bush foods. A couple of years later, he led an expedition retracing the journals of explorer Christie Palmerston (1850?–1897) in the North Queensland rainforests.

Respected as a consummate bushman, Palmerston was on unusually close terms with the aboriginals, whose allegiance he won with his firmness and skill as a shot. Although he was ostensibly searching for gold, Palmerston's bush skills were legendary, and he spent many years in the Australian jungle and its outskirts, becoming one of the country's greatest explorers and aboriginal experts in a period when white contact was in its infancy. By travelling in Palmerston's footsteps, Les

Left: *Les Hiddins in the Daintree Rainforest. He is very comfortable there and very knowledgeable about the area's plants and animals.*

was able to hone his bush skills, and unlock the secrets of the Queensland rainforests for a whole new generation of enthusiasts.

In 1987 Les was awarded a Defence Fellowship to research survival in northern Australia. He was the principal author of the Australian Army's *Combat Survival Manual* (1987) and was awarded the Order of Australia Medal (AM) in 1987. His research was turned into a hit TV series *Bush Tucker Man*, which involved him driving around in a Land Rover Defender 110 with his trademark hat, finding and describing native Australian bush food. Les appeared in two ABC TV series of *Bush Tucker Man*, and the series *Bush Tucker Man – Stories of Survival*. He also appeared in countless TV documentaries, and wrote a number of books on survival, bush skills, the Queensland culture, geography, indigenous peoples and wildlife for adults and children.

Les retired from the Army in 1989 with the rank of major but continued to serve with the Army Reserve until 2001, working with aboriginal communities in northern Australia. Since 2001 Hiddins has been at the forefront of establishing wilderness retreats for war veterans. Pandanus Park, the flagship for these retreats, is a parcel of Normanby River frontage on Kalpowar Station, adjoining Lakefield National Park in Cape York. Here, veterans suffering from post-traumatic stress disorder and other problems associated with post-war life are encouraged to test their survival skills and camp in the bush, free of bureaucracy and regulations – keeping active rather than sitting around.

One of Les's greatest achievements was to produce something called 'snack maps'. At the suggestion of an army colleague, he compiled information about the wild foods that could be found in each part of the country, which would be essential for survival if a plane crash-landed, for example, and he arranged to have the information printed on the back of a map. Army men are notorious for cutting up maps into small pieces to use in specific areas, and, ingeniously, Les managed to get the appropriate information on the back of every map section, so that it related to the specific geographical areas on the other side.

Now retired, Les is still impassioned by the bush, and was all too willing to join me on an expedition from the eastern coast of Queensland into its heart and beyond, in which we would pool our knowledge of survival techniques and I would learn from his vast expertise about Australian bush food.

Bush tucker is Australian terminology for the huge variety of herbs, spices, fungi, fruits, flowers, vegetables, animals, birds, reptiles and insects that are native to the continent. Indigenous people have survived on the land for more than 50,000 years – some say many thousands of years more. In colonial times, pioneering white settlers who adopted aboriginal knowledge of local foods fared better than those who did not, but it took a brave man to stomach some of the offerings, and to get to grips with aboriginal cooking methods – many of which were designed to make a food safe to eat rather than more palatable. Les and I planned to use this age-old wisdom to travel through the area together, and we combined our knowledge and tricks to great effect. What better way to learn the tricks of Australian bush tucker than from the Bush Tucker Man himself?

We started in the Australian Daintree Rainforest, on the east coast of Queensland, which is over 135 million years old. Teeming with wildlife and flora, it's home to the largest range of plants and animals of any ecosystem on earth, with the highest number of rare or threatened species in the world. Some 430 species of bird live among the trees, including thirteen species found nowhere else in the world.

While some of these plants provide sustenance, others are dangerous and must be avoided. Take, for example, the wait-awhile vine. Its thin strands are covered with small spikes that grab clothing, rip at skin, and generally tear up anything that comes within reach of them. These vines hang from large trees to the rainforest floor and can be found in thick clumps in places.

Another plant to be wary of is the giant stinging tree (known as gympie gympie). It has large leaves that look harmless, but they are covered with thousands of microscopic pricks that, if touched, embed themselves into your skin, causing indescribable pain and itching. They can even penetrate rubber gloves. And once stung, there isn't much you can do but pay a visit (by air) to the closest hospital. Les explained that the hollow pricks are unbelievably insidious, causing a reaction that lasts up to six months – or even more. The pricks affect the nervous system, making contact with anything hot or cold excruciatingly painful. Sufferers have to shave off the pricks and then coat the site with a latex substance that stops air getting to the skin. Even dead leaves still have venomous stingers so they should be avoided at all costs, no matter what your protection.

Interestingly, the fruit of the stinging tree, which looks a little like a raspberry, is edible but it tastes watery and insipid. You have to brush off the very fine hairs on them, which can give a mild sting. I tried some on camera but I wouldn't recommend it because if the hairs sting your throat, it could swell up and cause you to die.

The blue quandong is a bizarre, olive-sized fruit with green, plum-like flesh and a beautiful pitted stone that is carved into earrings and other *objets d'art* by local craftsmen. It's known as a 'wild peach', and the tree itself grows up to 35 metres in height. The fruit tastes a little like an English hawthorn berry. Loggers targeted this tree in the past because of its pale timber, and as a consequence it was over-harvested at one stage. The fruit ripens between August and January, so if you are travelling in these months, you can sample its delights – although you may have to fight off indigenous birds and reptiles to get there first. Local populations still rely on its fruit, as it is an excellent source of vitamin C and fibre.

When Les and I were up on the Roper River in the Northern Territory, we sampled the native grapes known as 'beer grapes'. These have three seeds inside and are a great source of nutrients but they can burn the back of the throat. Les showed me that by picking them from trees with their roots in water, you can find specimens with a less intense taste that are quite palatable. In fact, you can judge a beer grape by how many beers you have to drink afterwards to take the taste away.

Les introduced me to the candlenut, probably the oiliest nut known to man. They cause diarrhoea unless well cooked, although Les and a colleague tested them out to see how many could be eaten raw before

Top right: *Avoid touching the giant stinging tree at all costs. The fruits are edible but not really worth the trouble.*

Right: *The blue quandong is an important bush food. The berries taste like hawthorn berries and are a good source of vitamin C.*

symptoms set in, and the answer is eight! They are a good source of protein and, importantly, fat, which can be in short supply in a bush tucker diet. They can also be used to make a candle because of their rich oils – hence their name.

One of the most important flowering trees in tropical rainforest is the fig – in fact, figs are considered to be a 'keystone species'. They produce fruit at different times of the year, providing a reliable food resource for many animals and birds all year round. One especially useful fig is the Round-leaf Banana fig (*Ficus crassipes*). It is most common at high altitudes in closed forest, but also occurs in coastal forests. With its dense, rounded canopy, familiar rubber-tree shaped leaves and squat, colourful fruit, it is attractive and easy to identify.

Traditionally, aboriginals looked at all food as medicine, and used different parts of plants and animals to keep them healthy and to prevent and treat illnesses. The plants indigenous to a region are frequently useful for treating health problems that occur in that region. For example, many rainforest fruits and plants have anti-fungal and anti-bacterial action, which is useful because bacterial and fungal infections naturally thrive in the hot, moist environment.

However, you have to be careful because some plants that look as though they could be edible are, in fact, highly toxic. The Burrawang palm is a member of the cycad family, and produces seeds that look delicious. They are edible by some animals but can lay a man out flat in just a few hours. Wild ginger is another tricky one: while some members of this family are a natural source of drinking water for travellers (you chop the ginger near the ground so that water drains out the stem), others contain poison. We cooked a fish wrapped in ginger leaves and they imparted a delicate ginger flavour to the flesh but unless you know what you are doing, and you have an intimate knowledge of ginger plants, give them a wide berth.

When I was in Arnhem Land in 1996 I came across another example of plants that can be poisonous if you don't prepare them properly. They have two types of yam – the long yam and the cheeky yam. You dig them up, clean them and cook them over coals for about two hours. After this time, the long yam will make a deliciously creamy dish, but the cheeky yam is still toxic.

It needs to be peeled, grated and left in a billabong overnight so that the toxins leach out, and by the following morning they are safe to eat – and very nutritious.

It might sound like a lot of bother in order to get a meal – but food is a precious resource in the bush. You need knowledge and expertise to find and prepare it, though, or you could make yourself very sick indeed.

Drinking water is normally plentiful in Queensland, with rushing rivers, streams and waterfalls. Some of these dry out during the dry season, and inland many are tainted with salt water; however, the magnificent trees of the rainforest hold plenty of water in their canopy of leaves, and edible fruits and plants provided liquids when we found ourselves further away from fresh-water sources.

The streams and rivers also provide a wealth of fish and crustaceans, particularly during the wet, warm seasons. During the colder season, the water temperature drops and fish swim closer to the surface and are therefore easier to catch, but they tend to be smaller and less plentiful. When we were up on the Roper River, Les and I dined on some amazing crayfish and freshwater mussels, which were easily caught in the shallows. Look for overhanging vegetation and soft sandy banks, and you are likely to find a veritable feast on the shores.

Seventy-eight of Australia's 190 species of fish live here. One of the most common families is the rainbowfish, which is found throughout the area, except around Cape Tribulation. Another widely distributed small fish is the Pacific blue-eye. Larger species found in the coastal reaches of the rivers include jungle perch, catfish, sooty grunter and mangrove jack. Barramundi is found from the rapids of the upper reaches of the rainforest rivers to the rocky headlands adjacent to the river mouths. They vary in size and distribution according to the time of year, salinity levels and water temperature, and can reach almost 20 kilograms in weight.

When fishing, though, remember to watch out for crocodiles. The estuarine crocodile is a saltwater croc, which can survive in both fresh and salt water, and they are plentiful in the rainforest region. An average adult male is typically 4.8 to 5 metres long, and weighs roughly 770 kilograms. These reptiles are fast. Often confused with freshwater crocodiles, who are far less dangerous, and after whom the 'Alligator rivers' in Arnhem Land were misnamed, the 'salties' are big and incredibly fast. They normally wait near the river bank – on land, or under the water (watch for the dual stream of bubbles from their nostrils; no other underwater creature has two nostrils from which to exhale air) – and pounce, thrashing their victims and dragging them underwater, often beneath a ledge or rock to 'soften' before they are eaten.

Not much escapes the appetite of an estuarine croc – fish, crabs, insects, turtles, birds, reptiles, dingoes, wallabies, domestic cattle and people are all attractive prey. Even the indigenous peoples have a healthy fear of these beasts, and take great care to avoid them – particularly in the wet season, when they become more plentiful inland. The year before my trip to Arnhem Land, an eight-year-old aboriginal child had been the victim of a crocodile attack in the area I visited. In their own environment, everything is in their favour. They're incredibly well camouflaged, they're fast and patient, and can be very fast-moving when they turn predator. They can creep up on you so quietly, you won't even know they are there.

You have to be very, very careful when travelling in northern Australia. That means, in the first instance, always remembering that crocodiles might be around. Never swim in any areas likely to have saltwater crocodiles. Never go near the water in the same place twice, and never bend over the water with your bucket – throw it out on a rope, and draw it in. Watch out when you are searching for shellfish. Get in and out quickly, and watch out for a crocodile ambush, and their telltale bubbles. Remember, too, that many crocs stray from the rivers, and you can come across one in dense bush. Like so many predators, they are more dangerous after dark, so it's not a good time to be moving about.

Fishing can also be a problem, as hungry crocodiles watch the proceedings carefully, as if to decide whether fisherman or fish will be the best prize. If you see a crocodile while fishing, sit very still and wait until he loses interest. Whatever you do, don't lean over the side of the boat or, if you are on shore, across the water.

You may also have to watch out for the box jellyfish, which congregate around the coastal areas, in shallow waters and in the mouths of estuaries, creeks, rivers and mangrove swamps, where they breed. Although they rarely venture inland, it's not unheard of. Box jellyfish are pale blue and transparent and bell- or cube-shaped with four distinct sides, hence the name 'box' jellyfish. Measuring up to 20 centimetres along each side of the cube or bell, the box jellyfish has up to fifteen tentacles on each corner which can be 3 metres in length. It shoots itself along in a jet-like motion and can administer a sting that causes searing pain and leaves prominent scars. If severe enough, stings can be fatal. Many swimmers drown after being stung, because they go into shock as a result of the pain. Box jellyfish breed in mangrove swamps and they are more numerous after rain, which flushes them out of river systems towards beaches. If stung, you should pour vinegar straight onto the wound (tourist beaches often have buckets of vinegar on standby), after which the tentacles can be removed, but you should then head straight to hospital for professional treatment. These are lethal creatures, and anywhere near coastal reaches can be home to them, particularly during the onset of the wet season across the top of northern Australia from October to March.

It's possible to have an extremely healthy diet in the rainforests, as long as you know what you are doing, and even in the dry seasons, when fish and other wildlife are less prolific, you can normally find something to eat. But don't be tempted to go it alone; you should only ever travel in these regions with an extremely experienced guide.

The wildlife of the rainforest floor is just as varied as its rivers and creeks, and can provide a meal if need be – but some species are dangerous so it's best to be on guard.

The cassowary is a large bird, about 1.5 metres tall, with a black body and a light blue head that darkens down the neck. There is a horny casque on top of the head that helps it to forge a path through dense forest. Two swinging red wattles hang from the throat and there is an orange patch on the back of the neck. This flightless bird is normally harmless and will probably run away

if it sees you, but if it feels under attack, it can lash out with sharp claws.

Feral pigs thrash through the rainforest, eating large quantities of native trees and animals. Current wild pig populations originated from domestic pigs that escaped from 19th-century European settlements. It is estimated that there are between 13 and 23 million feral pigs spread across the Australian continent. Adult males have been known to reach 1.8 metres in length and weigh up to 300 kilograms, so they can pose a threat if you are in the wrong place at the wrong time, and they may eat dogs and other small mammals. They spread the root-rot fungus with their hoofs, and have been declared a pest by the Australian National Parks authorities – largely because they destroy the natural habitats of native species, decimate crops and spread noxious weeds.

One of the most fascinating creatures to behold is the brush-turkey, a relative of the mallee fowl and the orange-footed scrubfowl, known as mound-builders or 'megapodes'. Brush-turkeys live in rainforest near the coast and in scrub further inland. They spend most of their time on the ground but roost in trees at night.

The male brush-turkey builds a mound of plant litter and soil, usually about 2 to 4 metres across and at least a metre high – but we saw some that were almost three times that size. They looked almost like miniature volcanoes. The male spends many hours building his mound and adding or removing material to keep it at a constant inside temperature of 33°C. He has highly accurate heat sensors in his bill, which he will poke inside the mound to check the temperature. When it is too hot, the male will rake material off the top to allow heat to escape. If it's too cold, the male will heap more material onto the mound to build its insulation. Male

Previous pages: *Les Hiddins and me at Bloomfield Falls, in the Daintree Rainforest.*

Right: *The butcher bird is very gregarious and will come down to your camp to steal food if you give it the opportunity.*

Above: *Bush hens and brush-turkeys incubate their eggs in these mounds, keeping the temperature constant by removing or adding layers of insulation.*

Left: *A green ants' nest. The camera crew got covered in green ants while we were shooting, which was very funny!*

brush-turkeys will defend their mounds and will only allow females onto the mounds when they are at exactly the right temperature.

Once the mound is at 33°C, females will return many times to mate and lay eggs. Eggs are put into holes about half a metre deep in the mound and then covered. Between eighteen and 24 eggs are laid in each batch and they take about 50 days to hatch. In the past, these eggs and the fowl themselves were a staple part of an aboriginal diet, but today the brush-turkeys (and their cousins, scrub hens) are protected by law.

Green ants are a local delicacy and an interesting source of bush medicine. Their torsos are green and they taste lemony. They're also known as weaver ants, as they weave together a nest out of leaves. Nests are oval in shape and can be up to 50 centimetres long but are more usually about 30 centimetres across. Because they are made from the leaves of the plant it is constructed in, they are well camouflaged and hard to see. One colony can have any number of 'individual' nests in a group of trees. Weaver ants will attack perceived intruders to defend their nest. Though they do not have a sting, after biting their enemy they secrete an acid (venom) from the tip of their abdomen into the wound to cause discomfort and irritation. They hold their abdomen high in the air in aggressive posture. If you break open their nest, you can remove a glutinous substance comprised of the larvae and the queen egg, which can be eaten or decocted to treat colds, bacterial infections, mouth ulcers, sinus infections, sore throats, and more. Oil from their abdomen has also been used by indigenous aboriginal people for sweetening water. Researchers have found that they contain vitamin C, which might be one reason why they are used successfully to ward off and treat colds. A number of studies are currently taking place into these green ants, who don't appear to suffer from any type of bacterial infection, and the findings could have some interesting applications for human medicine.

These are only a few of the huge number of flora and fauna indigenous to the rainforest, and at first glance it may seem that survival in its depths would be easy given such a wide range of food sources – but don't be fooled. You have to know what you are doing, or living off the land is nigh on impossible. It's difficult to track and catch wildlife – many species are camouflaged by the overgrowth of plants, and many of these plants have defences to protect themselves from predators, which can be life-threatening to unsuspecting travellers. Programmes like mine and Les's make survival in the bush look easy, but that's because we've got decades of experience behind us and we know our subjects inside and out.

Finding shelter isn't difficult in the rainforest, but you have to set up your camp carefully to deter predators and protect yourself from insects, spiders and snakes. The buttresses of trees – distinctive flanges at the bases – can provide terrific shelter from rain. Trees are buttressed only in tropical and subtropical forests. Buttressing probably helps them to breathe in water-logged soils or take up nutrients from shallow soils.

I entered the rainforest with my ubiquitous 'swag', which is basically a good-quality foam mattress inside a canvas cover that encloses both the bedding and the sleeper. Traditionally blankets were used, but sleeping-bags are more practical when it's very cold. You can wrap up your pillow and duvet or blankets in the swag as well. The swag is rolled and fastened with straps, and it's easy to unroll when you reach your camp. Mine has an intrinsic net cover – essential in any areas where insects are a problem. Many travellers make the mistake of buying cheap mosquito nets, but unless your mesh is incredibly dense, you still risk attack from sandflies and other small insects, who make short work of invading any net that doesn't have minute holes. In the rainforest, or during the rainy season in any part of the continent, you'll need a tarpaulin to protect you from the elements.

In Arnhem Land, I learned a technique of keeping insects away by lighting a small fire under your shelter. It is a bit odd sleeping in smoke, but it's effective. Make a fire in the inside of a red termite mound, which is a slow burner that produces just the right amount of smoke. In an emergency, you can improvise some mosquito netting with old flour bags or any tightly woven fabric, but it is far better to travel with your own mosquito net and insecticides to be on the safe side.

Indigenous populations lived in temporary dome huts thatched with paperbark, which could be easily built and then discarded if weather

Above: *The traditional way of camping in the rainforest would be with a tarp and a swag, and mosquito net pegged down all round.*

Right: *A modern swag with built-in tight mesh, which is good for keeping out sandflies.*

Above: *If you light a fire in a tree buttress, keep it small to avoid damaging the tree. It's a convenient option because you can suspend your billycan from a stick balanced across the buttress rather than hammering stakes into the ground. You also use less firewood because it's less draughty meaning the wood burns more efficiently. Bushcraft is all about taking the simple solution.*

conditions changed. For example, if a sudden downpour of rain threatened to raise river levels and flood a camp, they could gather together their few belongings and move to a more suitable place where a new camp would be built quickly and simply.

Another thing to watch out for when camping are dingoes. I warned my crew not to leave their shoes out at night or they might be taken by these native dogs. They're crafty little animals, and have been known to take everything from camping goods to small children. The dingo – Australia's only native dog – is thought to have descended from a family of wild Asian dogs. They are Australia's largest meat-eater and hunt many other animals, including the kangaroo. Unable to bark, the dingo howls at night to keep the family group together and to warn others to stay away. Highly adaptable, they live everywhere from arid deserts to lush rainforests, and inhabit every Australian state apart from Tasmania. Watch out – they are stealthy, and they can bite. And they like shoes.

No matter how you are camping or travelling, making a fire is a must – but it's not always easy work. Even aboriginals tend to carry burning embers with them from camp to camp. The most seasoned tracker or camper would struggle to create a fire using friction in wet weather. You need particular types of wood or you will get blisters on your hands long before you create a spark. I like to find a dry branch in the undergrowth and, using a machete, quickly carve off thin slivers so that they ignite more easily.

Near the Roper River, I found a fungus called *Daldinia sp.* (also known as coal fungus or carbon balls) that can be used to start a fire. It is usually attached to dead or decaying trees, is very hard and carbonaceous, much like a lump of coal, and is fantastic as tinder for a fire. It does need to be completely dry, but will easily take a spark from a flint. It burns slowly, much like a charcoal briquette, with a particularly pungent smoke. Once lit it is quite difficult to extinguish, but fragments can be broken off and transferred to a tinder ball to create an open flame. It's invaluable in the bush, or any other place in the world where it's difficult to start a fire, and because it is a slow burner, an ignited 'ball' can be taken with you, often for days, as a fire starter.

An old Australian method of hanging your billycan over a fire is to make a tripod shape with three sticks and place a tin can on top. Make a hole in the can and suspend a piece of wire with a hook on it through the middle. You will hang your billycan or cooking pot from the hook. Adjust the length of the wire so that your can just sits neatly above the flames, letting your water come to the boil. Alternatively, use a tree buttress to hang your billycan over a fire – the outreach of the tree prevents the fire from building too quickly.

Les and I set out towards the Little Eva crash site – a long, tiring, off-road journey across an incredibly varied landscape. We were exhausted by almost monotonous driving in modern vehicles, even though the scenery was breathtaking. It provided a stark reminder of what it must be like to be stranded in the Australian bush – miles of dense scrub, much of it looking the same, which provides little or no clue as to the part of the country you are in. The journeys of explorer Friedrich Wilhelm Ludwig Leichhardt (see pages 35–36) have captured the imagination of many, both in his own time and in the century and a half since he began his expeditions through Queensland, and we decided to follow his footsteps into the bush for part of the way (see the map on page 18 for his route). He travelled nearly 5,000 kilometres from the eastern Queensland coast to Port Essington, east of Darwin, losing many of his team en route, but nonetheless achieving his goal of surviving the rugged, inhospitable Australian bush in Gulf Country.

The coast of the Gulf of Carpentaria has some of Australia's wildest and most remote country. Before early explorers returned from the area with tales of unparalleled hardships, there was a plan to build a port here where merchants could trade with Asia. However,

Right: *An improvised pot hanger using an old tin can and a piece of wire: very simple, very effective.*

the terrain made any such plan impossible. The Gulf coast is interlaced with hundreds of drainage channels carrying wet season rains away from the flat country further inland. The flatness of this inland terrain causes the water to sweep across the plains in sheets, or thousands of tiny rivulets, rather than being directed into one or two major rivers. In mountainous country, rivers run only into each other. Here, the land is so flat that water flows out into two or more forks from the one source. This constant fanning out of watercourses, combined with a sheltered coastline and a tropical climate, results in a twisting, jungle-lined delta – utterly inaccessible by an overland route to this day. Rain can make this arid region bloom, but it's a land of sparse population, long empty roads and tiny distant settlements.

The Gulf Country covers an area of approximately 425,000 square kilometres and encompasses a great variety of environments, from the rocky uplands around Mount Isa to the rich bluegrass flats which extend from the most southerly point of the Gulf. Rainfall in the region generally decreases from north to south and east to west. It straddles Queensland and the Northern Territory, and although parts of it today are used for grazing, it is largely unpopulated and impossible to negotiate – not just because of dense scrub, but also because of the myriad waterways, which criss-cross the landscape.

Little Eva crashed way to the west of Burketown, which is even today a very isolated town located on the Albert River and Savannah Way in an area known as the Gulf Savannah. Extending from the Great Dividing Range in the east to the Northern Territory border in the west, the Gulf Savannah region is a dry country, subject to regular cyclones, bush fires and drought. The town was named in honour of ill-fated explorer Robert O'Hara Burke,

Left: *Having a brew at the end of the day in northern Queensland. I really like this country.*

149

following his overland expedition in 1861 (see pages 36–39).

The area is characterised by hot, humid and wet summers and warm, dry winters. December is the hottest month, with average maximum temperatures rising to 35.5° C and rainfall is heaviest during the months of January and February. Flooding, often associated with the passage of a tropical cyclone, can isolate communities for months, even today. This is true outback, with vivid red desert sand dunes, eucalyptus coolabah-lined rivers, rocky outcrops, dinosaur fossil sites, and thorny scrubland. In some places, we struggled to see just a metre or so ahead of us, and the land, at every turn, looks identical. The prospect of being lost in this territory is overwhelming. In every direction there is heat, scrub, arid land, and dense wilderness.

After thousands of miles of cross-country driving, Les and I helicoptered out to the site of the Little Eva wreckage. It's so remote that travelling by land was out of the question. Even though we had a crew and proper backup, I insisted that we took with us two days' worth of food and water, plus satellite phones and GPS navigational equipment. I don't normally do that but the remoteness of the country is serious enough to focus the mind so that you don't take any chances.

Landing was difficult, as there is so little groundspace unoccupied by thick, hard and thorny plantlife. Once on the ground, we spent several hours clearing a landing strip for the crew who were supposed to be following on behind.

We looked up into the sky, but there was no sign of them and after an hour or so, we started to become worried. We eventually managed to contact them by phone, and it turned out that the helicopter pilot had been sleeping

Previous pages: *You can see how well the Little Eva crash site was hidden by the bush. If you walk 10 metres in any direction you can't spot it any more. It's no surprise that it took rescuers six weeks to find it, and amazing that they managed it at all.*

Right: *A close-up of the crash site. The engines have been stripped out but otherwise it looks just as it did when it came down.*

beside his helicopter the night before, and hadn't put out his fire properly. When he tried to take off, the downdraft ignited the brush, starting a massive bush fire that they had to fight to put out. It's a tough country, and easy to get things wrong. It was an eerie feeling being cut off while we waited for our late arrivals – a tiny taste of what the Little Eva survivors experienced for months on end.

This is a story that could be told and retold for centuries without losing its impact, and I for one am fascinated by it. You really have to see this landscape to appreciate how hard survival must have been for men who were not only completely untrained in survival, but who knew little or nothing about the landscape, the geography of the continent, and the wildlife that might have saved them. I am indebted to Barry Ralph's book *Savage Wilderness* (2004) for much of the story that follows and recommend that you read it if you want to learn more.

On 2 December 1942, a US Air Force Liberator known as Little Eva and four other B24 planes had taken part in a high-level bombing campaign against a Japanese convoy of supply ships, some 80 kilometres north of the northern tip of Queensland. They had a secret airbase there at Iron Range, in a perfect location for bombing Japanese troops in New Guinea. On the day in question, the Little Eva crew got separated from the others and couldn't find their target, so they ended up ditching their bombs into the sea – something that airmen like to avoid at all costs, partly because it represents failure.

On their return journey, they were caught up in a severe tropical thunderstorm. By all accounts, the pilot achieved a miracle by pulling off a remarkable manoeuvre, that had never been achieved in a Liberator before, to save them after the plane entered a nose dive. The radios went dead and, no longer hearing the sound of their engines, the captain, Lieutenant Crosson, ordered his crew of nine to bail out. He probably thought they were somewhere in the region of Cairns, on the coast south of the airbase. In fact, they were hundreds of kilometres to the west, in land that was and still is largely uncharted.

The first four men – Grimes, Speltz, Gaston and Dyer – bailed out, followed by Crosson and crew-member Wilson. Crosson and Wilson came down about 3 kilometres from the crash site, and walked back to it. They were met with a distressing sight – the plane was still burning and four crew members

Above: *The side gunner's door, where Charles Workman's parachute got stuck. Crosson and Wilson found him dangling here while three other crew members had burned to death inside.*

(McKeon, Hilton, Gurdas and Workman) had been killed when it crashed. Workman's parachute had caught in the doorway, and he'd been beaten to death on the tail section of the aircraft. Either the others had been trying to help Workman untangle his chute, or they'd decided not to jump and take their chances in the crash. Bullets were exploding, and anything that might have been useful in terms of provisions or protection was destroyed. Crosson and Wilson decided to wait there a while for the others to join them.

Above: *The wreck still contains recognisable bits of military equipment. Let's hope people leave them for generations to come. There's a real aura of tragedy there that I think should stay undisturbed. It's not a place to visit lightly, as it's reached via a long bush journey followed by a helicopter flight.*

Twenty kilometres to the north, the four other survivors landed. Having seen the coastline before they landed, it's likely they thought they were somewhere on the Cape York coast, and they decided against walking towards the burning crash site, instead heading north towards the coast, where they probably believed their airbase and settlements were located. Anyone with survival skills knows that when you come down in that part of Australia you always head east, where civilisation is. However, their unfamiliarity with the landscape and the country, and their disorientation, led them in the opposite direction, straight into some of the most dangerous and isolated parts of the continent. A few miles away to the east they might have come across Burketown – by no means a sprawling conurbation, but certainly a place from which they would be rescued. Between these four survivors they had four bars of chocolate, a jungle knife, a fish hook and fishing line, and a few matches. They were just eighteen years old, they'd just survived a plane crash and they had no survival equipment.

Crosson and Wilson eventually gave up waiting at the crash site, and headed east where thirteen days later, on 14 December, they bumped into the manager of Escott cattle station, 15 kilometres west of Burketown. They had survived with very little food and water, living on raw fish and scavenged meat. Their feet were badly blistered, they were burned from the unremitting sun, and suffering from severe hunger and exhaustion.

Sadly, Crosson and Wilson couldn't pinpoint the exact location of the crash site on a map. For several days, US flight command control didn't even realise that the plane was missing. Low-flying aircraft were eventually sent out to find the wreckage and try to locate the survivors, but the men on the ground had no means of signalling and the dense brush made it impossible for them to make themselves known. Gaston later recalled seeing three B24s crossing at an altitude of about 1,000 feet overhead, about a week before Christmas 1942, but their attempts to signal to it were fruitless.

A rescue was mounted from Burketown, using the best bushmen in the area, and it took them six weeks to find the aircraft – located some 64 kilometres from Escott Station. Air force intelligence was extremely concerned that the site be discovered, and that all secret bombs removed. Sadly, army secrecy was one of the reasons why the search for survivors was so late in getting off the ground, and so poorly organised. Their primary goal was to ensure that the crash site held no secrets that might provide an advantage to the enemy. When they reached the site, they buried the bodies of the four airmen in a shallow grave. They have since been removed.

The bushmen picked up the trail of the remaining survivors, thanks largely to the efforts of Grady Gaston, who had manned the plane's ball turret. He kept making marks as they travelled, breaking branches and twigs, and leaving articles behind in the hope that they would eventually be traced. At one stage, rescuers found Hilton's leather jacket floating in a creek, and later they found part of a chopped-up lifejacket that they guessed the survivors had been using as a water-carrier.

Fate, however, was not on their side. This was the rainy season, a truly horrendous time to be lost in the bush. Of the horses on which the search party rode, one was bitten by a King Brown snake and another was stung by a wasp and impaled itself on a tree trying to get away, meaning that both had to be shot. Eventually, the search party was forced to turn back and resupply. They set out again and found traces of the four men, but once again struggled with the hostile terrain and were forced back. All of the bushmen suffered from severe exhaustion and were dispirited. You have to see this country to believe it.

The search party persisted for over 130 kilometres. In the wet conditions they would often lose the tracks, particularly when crossing streams, but they picked them up again until they eventually lost them completely at Settlement Creek, just short of the Queensland/Northern Territory border. Finding no tracks on the other side of the creek, they assumed the survivors must have been the victims of crocodiles. The search party returned to Burketown and the search was called off. The US Air Force continued to search Gulf Country from the air but they could turn up nothing.

So where were they? After landing, Gaston and his three companions walked to the coastline of the Gulf of Carpentaria, which they struggled to follow in a westerly direction. They sucked on leaves and chewed on green bark to quench their thirst, and dodged crocodile-infested rivers to make their way to what they thought was safety. On the fourth day after the crash, they shot and killed a young bullock with one of the two handguns they had with them. Their matches were too damp to light a fire so they had to eat the flesh raw. They didn't take any of the meat with them, something they would go on to regret as just a day later, their guns had rusted so much in the humid conditions that they were entirely useless and had to be discarded. The fast-flowing rivers were difficult to negotiate, and shallow crossings were few and far between. It's amazing that none of them was eaten by the many crocodiles in the region, particularly when they were waist-deep in the mud. The territory they traversed ranged from dense scrubland to muddy bogs, and then impenetrable tropical jungle.

They crossed Settlement Creek, where the search party lost their trail. On 24 December, the men thought they were nearing rescue when they found a small paperbark shack, but it proved to be deserted. A watermelon vine at the site was, however, an unexpected bonus, and they feasted that night, singing Christmas carols and saying Christmas prayers in the hope that rescue was nigh. Unfortunately, the seasonal weather put paid to all their hopes, and it rained heavily for several days afterwards. Speltz's feet were in poor condition and he couldn't walk any further, so the others left him in the shack to head north-west looking for a homestead. They reached the Robinson River, which was swollen from the heavy rain. Dyer waded across first, then Gaston, both nervous of the depth of the water and the strength of the current. They reached the opposite bank and turned to watch in despair as Grimes disappeared under the water and was swept away. There was nothing they could do.

Dyer and Gaston continued for another 40 kilometres, along the shores of the Gulf of Carpentaria, but they were getting weaker by the day and succumbing to the symptoms of malnutrition, their wasting muscles making it harder to keep going. They decided to head back to the shack where they'd left Speltz, feeling very gloomy about their chances of rescue by now, and on the way back their spirits were further dashed when they came upon Grimes' body face down in the sand.

Once back in the shack, they took turns to forage for dead fish washed up on the sand, and fruits and berries gathered from trees. Gaston tried to lift the spirits of the others, but one day he and Speltz returned from a foraging trip to find that Dyer had died, sitting in the corner of the shack, holding a piece of bark on which he had scratched: 'I lasted till February 10.' Two weeks later, on 24 February, Speltz died in Gaston's arms.

Somehow Gaston carried on. His will to live must have been staggering. He later said that there were two things he wanted to do in his life – he wanted a girlfriend, and to buy a car – and this spurred him on to continue long after he'd lost his colleagues. He said that he survived mainly on raw snake; without the wherewithal to cook them, he was able nonetheless to trap them with forked sticks and survive for months with little else. Although water was in plentiful supply, some of it was salt water, which had infiltrated the coastal estuaries, and many sources were riddled with crocodiles. The swift currents and flooding made it difficult to get to the water he needed in some cases, and he had no means of hunting or fishing, having lost or discarded most of the items of any use.

Much of the local flora – some of it the very same offerings that Les and I found in the rainforest, and were often hard pressed to categorise, even half a century later – was potentially poisonous, and the airman struggled to find enough to eat. Native passion fruit came in season during the months he was there and then went back out again. Wildlife was driven out by the flooding and tumultuous weather conditions. In the scrub, even an expert like Les admits to struggling to find anything safe to eat.

One of the common side-effects of starvation is that it has a psychological impact, in particular increasing thoughts of defeat, of giving up. This alone makes Gaston's survival nearly unbelievable. He carried on well past the point of starvation, and into the beyond. One day, he found an abandoned spearhead and I imagine this must have lifted his spirits immeasurably, because it would enable him to hunt for larger prey such as rabbits. But as he got weaker, he was unable to venture far from the hut and he survived on sand crabs which he grabbed from the beach outside. Some dingoes began snapping at his heels whenever he went out, making him fearful that he would end up being eaten by them.

Above: *A bearded, painfully thin Grady Gaston after his rescue.*

Right: *Native passion fruit came into flower and then back out again over the period when Gaston was living in the shack.*

Eventually, long after the search had been called off, a stockman and four aboriginals arrived at the hut where they had been sheltering and immediately realised that someone had been staying there recently. An aboriginal tracker called Strike-a-Light was sent out to find him. In May 1943, 141 days after Little Eva crashed, Grady Gaston was rescued and taken to Seven Emu Station.

Gaston was a young man, still in his twenties, but he arrived gaunt, white-haired and dispirited. As one historian said, 'Finding Grady Gaston alive up to 200 miles from the crash site amounted to a miracle, but while the man may have survived the ordeal [he] did not survive the experience'. Gaston eventually returned to his home in the US, but suffered from a nervous disposition and various mental and physical health problems for the remainder of his life. If he had had proper counselling, a traumatic experience could have become a very positive one, but instead he was just sent home to deal with it as best he could.

Les and I discussed his journey and those of his colleagues at length, and although we could pinpoint errors they made in their attempts to be rescued, we remain stunned that they managed to survive for so long in such horrific conditions, and with virtually no knowledge of the land in which they had found themselves. The experience of these young American airmen validates what Les did later in the army – providing maps with tips for survival and nourishment in any part of the Australian continent. Sadly, his efforts came half a century too late for Gaston and his fellow airmen.

We realised that the only people who could survive such devastating conditions must not only be strong and brave, but they must also have an overwhelming determination to live. Gaston proved himself to be one such character, marking their paths, using his relentless optimism to drive his colleagues forward and even, when left alone, to continue until he reached his goal. His story is undoubtedly the stuff of legend, but it is also inspirational, and when you've had a bird's-eye view of the conditions in which Gaston survived, you can be nothing but humbled.

No one can underestimate the dangers of the Australian continent. A beautiful country, teeming with exquisite plant and animal life, it is, nonetheless, one of the most isolated parts of the earth. Even native populations have given it a wide berth, and for obvious reasons. The rainforest holds one set of hazards; the bushland still another. The arid desert is land that still defeats the most technologically advanced and knowledgeable travellers, and yet one man made it his mission to understand its parched depths, and with little more than a convoy of farm animals and minimal supplies, traverse it in record time. That man was John McDouall Stuart, and his journey across the red, sandy deserts of the Australian interior remain, to this day, another reminder of how man can fight the elements when he has a goal, the will to live, and an instinctive understanding of the land on which he's chosen to leave his mark. We'll go there next.

Right: *The terrain through which Grady Gaston walked for over 300 kilometres and stayed alive for 141 days.*

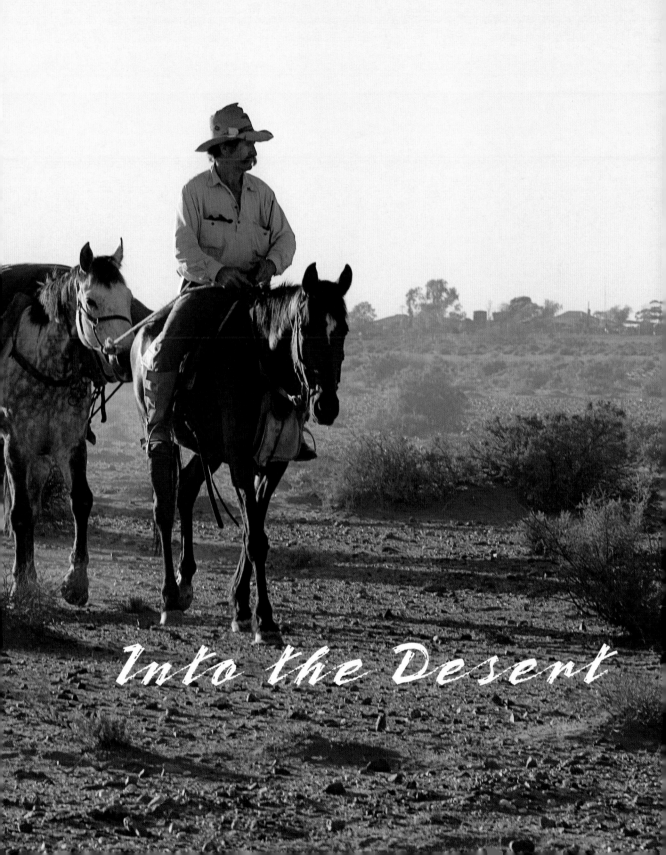

Into the Desert

The Australian desert is awe-inspiring in its beauty and ruthlessness. Many men have lost their lives in its depths and, even today, huge parts of it are completely desolate. Even indigenous people, plants and wildlife struggle to survive in its aridity. It is countryside that demands respect, as those who have successfully crossed and inhabited the dry, dusty terrain have been forced to acknowledge. There are a number of deserts in the Australian interior, each with different native plants and wildlife, and varying colours of sand, but all equally barren and unpredictable. I've come to love the desert, despite its difficulties, and there seemed no better way to investigate it for the *Walkabout* TV series than to follow in the footsteps of one of its greatest explorers, John McDouall Stuart.

Left: *John McDouall Stuart surveyed this hill for precious metals and left a cairn here. Using modern transport, we can do in a few hours what would have taken him months, but we have to go where there are roads, while his journeys on horseback weren't so restricted.*

Much of the interior of Australia is comprised of desert. Although deserts officially make up only 18 per cent of the total area of the landmass, 70 per cent of the country is classified as arid or semi-arid, which means that it gets less than 500 millimetres of rain per year, making Australia the driest inhabited continent on earth, second only to Antarctica. Only 3 per cent of the Australian population lives in the interior; the rest is concentrated on the coasts.

Deserts spread and regress across the years, depending upon rainfall. There are ten or eleven deserts in Australia – the Great Victoria, the Great Sandy, Tanami, Simpson, Gibson, Strzelecki, Little Sandy, Sturt Stony, Tirari and Pedirka deserts. The Western Desert is listed in some resources, but it is not officially recognised as a desert in its own right. Stuart crossed many of them in his travels.

We know he travelled through the Strzelecki Desert, which is located in South Australia, Queensland and New South Wales, and lies to the south-east of the Lake Eyre Basin, and north of the Flinders Ranges. This desert is characterised by extensive dune fields and is home to three wilderness areas.

Sturt's Stony Desert is an area in the north-east of South Australia, named by Charles Sturt in 1844 when he was trying to reach the exact centre of Australia. The stones caused his horses to limp and wore down the hoofs of the cattle and sheep that he had taken on the expedition. Stuart had the same trouble with horses on his later expeditions, and he learned to take along a blacksmith and plenty of spare horseshoes.

The Tanami Desert is in northern Australia. It has a rocky terrain with small hills and is one of the most isolated and arid places on earth. This desert was the Northern Territory's final frontier and wasn't fully explored until well into the 20th century. It is now traversed by the Tanami Track, but in the 1860s it was one of Stuart's major stumbling blocks.

Despite his careful charts and journals, we aren't entirely sure whether he crossed the Gibson Desert, which is covered by small sand dunes and a few

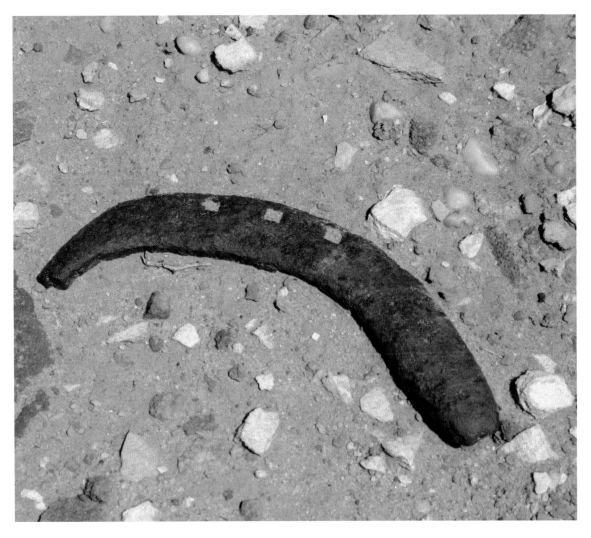

Above: *A broken horseshoe lying in the sand is testament to one of the huge problems Stuart faced in stony Gibber Country.*

Pages 168–9: *We followed wheel tracks that had been there for generations. Once this earth is compacted the imprints remain.*

Above: *Horses are still used to traverse the desert because they give good access to the country.*

rocky hills, and is home to numerous aboriginal reserves. It heads westward from the interior of the country and it's possible he may have touched upon its edges during some of his expeditions.

Stuart covered parts of the Great Victoria Desert, which stretched out from the western midlands into the centre of the southern part of the continent. Famous for its red sand dunes, indigenous wildlife and isolation, the Victoria Desert (400,000 square kilometres in size) is mainly a barren area of red sandhills and ridges, dry salt lakes, and very little grassland. Not surprisingly, Stuart found little water there. The red dunes had attracted early Australian prospectors and explorers, and although the desert's tip lies somewhere near Alice Springs, definitely in the south of the country, many travellers prior to Stuart believed they had found the continent's 'red centre' and were at least halfway to the northern coast.

Of course, most of these deserts had not been named during Stuart's time, and in several documents he refers to the 'great sandy desert', which has confused later historians. In fact, the Great Sandy Desert (perhaps later named) is a huge (240,000 square kilometre) desert south of the Kimberleys, and is characterised by scrub vegetation and rocks, as well as miles of red sand ridges and dunes. To this day few people traverse it, or live there.

At 90,000 square kilometres in size, the Simpson Desert, which lies to the north-east of the Great Victoria Desert, and directly in the path of Stuart's journeys, is comprised of sand drifts and wind-blown sand dunes. This was another problem area for Stuart because it receives very little rain and the summer heat can be particularly brutal. Temperatures often exceed 49° C, and humans are advised to be especially cautious here in summer.

All the Australian deserts are unforgiving territory, where even modern, well-equipped travellers can easily perish. In parts, it's almost like the surface of Mars, and NASA has tested equipment for Mars landings on its rocky surface. It's not completely barren or lifeless, but you definitely need specialist guidance out there to survive for any length of time.

The secrets of desert survival were, of course, the preserve of the aboriginals, who had adapted to the land over tens of thousands of years. Old people passed on the knowledge of where waterholes were located, and impressed on youngsters the responsibility for preserving those precious sites. They knew where edible plants might be located, how to track prey, and how to prepare and cook any foods they came across, so that they could survive on their own for weeks on end while crossing the desert. Although there is plentiful wildlife – such as feral camels, dingoes and goannas, red kangaroos (who live over most of the dry, inland, central part of Australia) and numerous species of lizard and bird – animals that live there tend to be heavily camouflaged, sometimes inedible, and often extremely elusive.

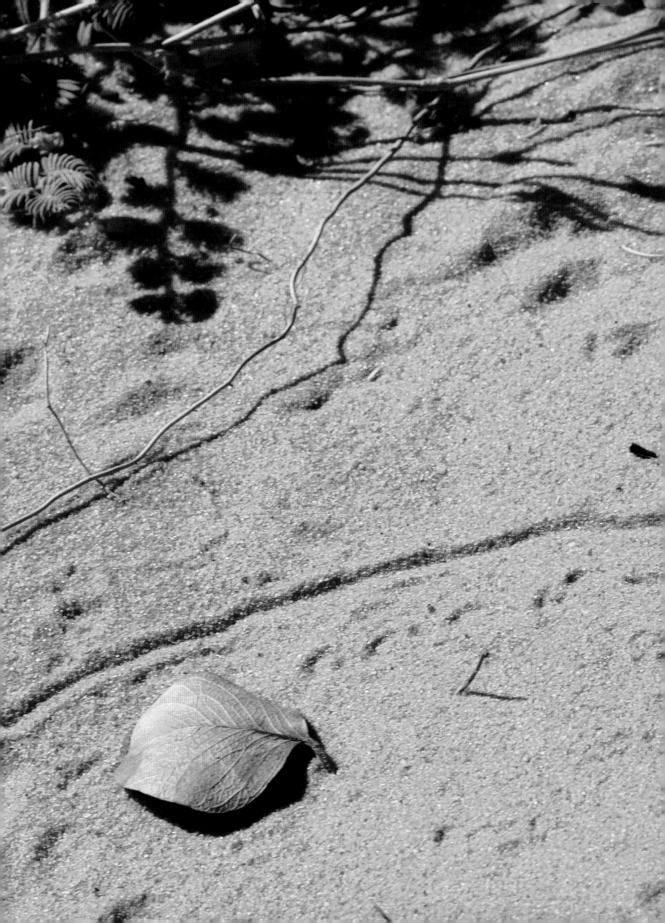

In intense heat most animals rarely emerge from their dens, and when they do, it is usually in the dead of night when cooler climes allow them to move freely without expending key resources.

Because of the low rainfall and the sandy surface, you can get very detailed knowledge of the activity of wildlife from tracks. Tracking involves a visual, sensual skill that is slowly dying out in the 21st century, but there is very little that escapes a properly trained aboriginal tracker. Back in the 1990s, when I was filming with the Pitjantjattara in the Central Desert, which is about the most difficult terrain you'll ever encounter, I worked with some aboriginal trackers and was very impressed by them. We were hunting emu and they shot one between the eyes and wounded another, which got away. From the blood trail, we knew we'd never catch it, but I said 'Come on, let's track it anyway,' and reluctantly they agreed. Those trackers picked up tiny disturbances, very, very fine signs that led us straight to the wounded bird and I knew I was working with top experts. Since then, I've come across other aboriginals who call themselves trackers and while they know enough to impress the tourists, they wouldn't dare to use the term in the company of old-timers.

Hunting in the desert was a serious business, a matter of life and death, and the eerie quiet made it essential that nothing would disturb the animals. For this reason, the aboriginals developed a type of sign language, in which they could signal to their fellow hunters without making a sound if there was a kangaroo, or a goanna or some other animal nearby. They were also expert at drawing shapes in the sand to illustrate their stories, replicating the footprints of various animals. The amazing thing is, of course, that these sand art stories can remain for years and years. Even heavy rain doesn't always erase the

Previous pages: *This type of sand records the finest details. Here we see a struggle as a wasp drags a caterpillar along. A good tracker would be able to look at the marks and tell exactly what had happened there.*

Right: *Aboriginals can make the prints of different kinds of animals – kangaroos, cats, dingoes and snakes – using the heel of the hand and the fingertips.*

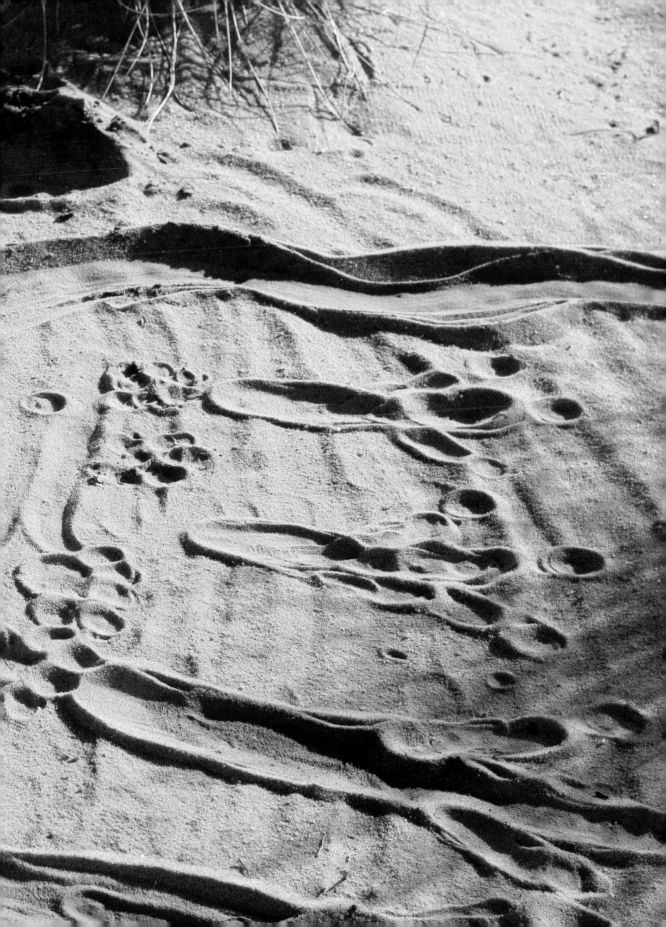

pictures, as they have been hardened into the sand by the intense heat, becoming something like stone upon which the water runs off.

Pat Lowe, the wife of aboriginal artist Jimmy Pike (see page 118) took me out into the Great Sandy Desert with her friends Jigadoo and Gunji, who were nomadic aboriginals until the 1970s, but had left the desert as children. I was intrigued as they showed me how the sand dunes recorded the past. The grains of sand are very, very fine, and even the smallest of creatures leave their mark. When we watched a wasp stinging a caterpillar and dragging it to its nest, the tracks told the whole story of the struggle for an experienced eye. Anyone would be inspired to learn tracking as a skill after an experience like this, and it's clear why the earliest aboriginals chose the sand and the rocks on which to relate their stories. It's interesting that crime in the desert is much lower than in other indigenous areas, largely because the criminals can't erase their tracks. They leave a lasting impression for long periods of time in this vast and arid land.

In her book, *Hunters and Trackers of the Australian Desert*, Pat wrote: '*Desert children used their fingers to trace out patterns and shapes. They also learned how to represent the tracks of common animals. Adults who grew up in the desert still enjoy demonstrating this game; the footprints of toddlers can be drawn with the heel of the hand and the fingertips; an eaglehawk's claws are "pinched" into the sand; a cat's paw is made with all the fingertips bunched together, and a dingo's pad with the flat of the finger pads. Finer marks, depicting the tracks of small birds and insects, can be drawn with a twig.*'

An experienced tracker can read the ground like a storybook; that's the way I learned to track. If the tracks are those of a mammal, a tracker can probably tell you,

Left: *The sign for an emu, top, and for a kangaroo, below.*

Above: *Shingleback lizards can supply up to 30 millilitres of fluid in their urine. It's not salty because they excrete salts through their skin. Watch they don't bite you, though. Their jaws are so strong that they will flatten a finger.*

from the size and 'weight' or depth of the tracks, its gender and approximate age. If the animal is a female, he will know by the spacing of her hind legs whether or not she is pregnant. He will also be able to tell you the species of a lizard and not only which way a snake is travelling, and its size, but how fast it is moving and whether it is harmless or venomous. She explains that while the King Brown and the black-headed python are snakes of similar size, their tracks are quite different. The python moves slowly, taking smaller 'strides' and leaving a shallow mark on the sand, while the King Brown moves more vigorously, with longer 'strides', leaving deeper marks.

Tracks in the sand aren't the only clue for trackers. Broken twigs, or dropped objects will also help them to follow a trail and allow them to judge how long it is since an animal has passed. Moist faeces will obviously be fresher than dry ones, and urine still damp on dry sand must have been sprayed very recently. Trackers can judge the type of bird or snake from its droppings: for example, the King Brown produces white faeces with a characteristic blue tinge. Pat says, 'I was once dissuaded from probing a hollow in a termite mound by the presence of blue-tinged droppings at the entrance.'

As we saw in the Early Explorers chapter, many explorers before Stuart depended heavily on the native populations for guidance. Stuart, however, preferred to use them occasionally, and to hone his own skills based on the knowledge that he accrued. It wasn't a consistently harmonious relationship. According to a story I was told by an aboriginal man called Reg Dodd, when Stuart was desperate in his search for water, he came across an aboriginal family who showed him a local waterhole. Stuart brought his horses to the hole and allowed them to drink it dry, which would have made him very unpopular. Aboriginals took great pains to ensure that their waterholes remained full and in good condition so that they would still provide a source of water for the next travellers to pass that spot. But the scale of Stuart's expeditions was such that he needed more resources than they could offer. There were a lot of problems he would have to solve for himself – and finding enough water for his horses as well as his men was paramount.

John McDouall Stuart was a small, lean and wiry man, with an insatiable addiction to exploration. He was a man who was much more comfortable in the outback than in society; someone who made repeated attempts to traverse the continent, returning on some occasions only to restock and renumber before setting out again. He was backed both by the government and members of the business community, all of whom had an interest in finding out about the Australian interior at a time when no claims had been made for much of her land or resources. Yet, it wasn't money or prestige that mattered to Stuart. He was an adept surveyor, a natural bushman and, by all accounts, one of the most instinctive explorers of the Australian continent. He'd experienced some early success in an expedition led by Sturt (see page 42), and he seems to have felt at his most confident in the bush, in pursuit of yet another challenge. He was a man who was undaunted by the elements, and despite suffering horrific physical degradation during his travels, continued until he had achieved his ultimate goal of travelling across Australia from south to north and back again – a feat that wasn't mastered by any of the other respected explorers and prospectors of that time.

Stuart was Scottish by birth, educated in Edinburgh and a pupil of the Scottish Naval and Military Academy, where many of his skills were honed; he graduated as a civil engineer. In January 1839 he emigrated to Southern Australia, at the age of 27, and quickly found work as a public surveyor. It's important to remember that Southern Australia was, at this time, nothing more than a pioneer outpost, with a series of tents and huts – a lifestyle fit only for the hardy and determined.

Right: *A statue commemorating Stuart in Adelaide. This is just outside the hotel in which we stayed, within sight of the Treasury, at the point from which he set off and to which he returned.*

JOHN M^c DOUALL STUART

EXPLORER

ADELAIDE TO INDIAN OCEAN

1861-2

I've always believed that it was partly Stuart's background as a Scotsman that helped to make him the man he was. His eventual explorations into the Australian interior were wrought with hardship, every trip characterised by dwindling resources and incredibly hostile elements, and yet he carried on with gritty Scottish determination. Rick Moore, president of the John McDouall Stuart Society in Australia, agrees that his birthplace may indeed have contributed to his success, confirming that a number of other key Australian explorers also hailed from Scotland.

When he lost his job as a public surveyor, Stuart simply found work as a private surveyor, soon becoming well known for his amazingly accurate work in remote scrublands. He took up farming, although he never really enjoyed the demands of working in the same place month after month. In 1844 he joined Captain Charles Sturt's expedition into the interior as a draughtsman. You may recall that Sturt had already 'solved the mystery' of the inland water systems of New South Wales, discovering the Darling River, travelling the full length of the Murrumbidgee, and tracing the Murray to the sea. Stuart was keen to join this legendary man in his search for the mythical 'inland sea'. It proved to be a devastatingly difficult journey. Instead of discovering waterways, they entered 'Sturt's Stony Desert', and then what is now known as the Simpson Desert – arid, formidable land that had never been navigated, and offered little in the way of sustenance. Second-in-command James Pool died of scurvy en route, and Stuart was appointed in his place. The men were stuck in the desert for six months, and upon their return were so ill that Sturt never truly recovered. He returned to England, while Stuart was unable to work or travel for over a year.

Top left: *Stuart's binoculars.*

Below left and right: *His compass with his name and the date engraved on the back.*

He eventually returned to his trade as a private surveyor, moving to Port Lincoln and then the northern Flinders Range, where he worked for wealthy pastoralists William Finke, and brothers John and James Chambers. He searched the countryside, surveying pastoral leases, and prospecting for minerals, his work funded by these backers who had a commercial interest in the land.

It was Finke who backed his first solo expedition, to find minerals and arable land in the north-west of Southern Australia, a land that was almost completely unexplored in the 1850s and is still unsettled today. He set off in May 1858 with two companions – a white man, Forster, and an aboriginal. Stuart was already advocating the merits of his unique contribution to Australian exploration – the concept of travelling 'light', and fast. The principle still holds true today when you're travelling in a 4x4. He took with him food and water for only six months, along with a compass, watch and half a dozen horses. While camels had often been used in bush exploration because of their low water requirements, Stuart put his faith in horses and used them throughout his career because, he said, he understood them better.

From the Flinders Ranges, Stuart travelled west to the south of Lake Torrens (a saline rift lake) and then north along its western edges. He travelled for four months, covering more than 2,000 kilometres, and discovering tracts of grazing land and a chain of semi-permanent waterholes that he named Chambers Creek (now called Stuart Creek). This would be a critically important staging post for later expeditions into Australia's 'red centre'. They wouldn't have found their way across otherwise.

He continued to the north-west, eventually reaching Coober Pedy (now known to be the site of rich opal fields), before lack of water and food for his men and his

Right: *Enough vitamin C for a man for a year. Stuart would only have needed two bottles of this to prevent the scurvy that was a major problem for his men.*

Above: *Chambers Creek. Imagine Stuart's excitement when he came across this chain of semi-permanent waterholes in the heart of the desert.*

horses forced him to turn towards the sea. On 7 August, he wrote in his journal:

'The journey to-day has been through horrid dense scrub and heavy sand hills Very little rain has fallen here, and we have been without water for the last two nights: the country is of such a light sandy soil that it will not retain it. I almost give up hopes of a good country; this is very disheartening after all that I have done to find it. If I see nothing from the top of the mount to-morrow, I must turn down to Fowler's Bay for water for the horses. As I could not remain quiet, I got on one of the lower spurs of Mount Finke to see what was before me. The prospect is gloomy in the extreme! I could see a long distance, but nothing met the eye save

A DENSE SCRUB AS BLACK AND DISMAL AS MIDNIGHT.'

The following day, he wrote: *'A FEARFUL COUNTRY. The whole of our journey to-day has been through a dreadful desert of sand hills and spinifex. In the last eight miles we have not seen a mouthful for the horses to eat and not a drop of water; it is even WORSE than Captain Sturt's desert, where there was a little salt bush; but here there is not a vestige.'*

He refers frequently to 'spinifex', which is a 'hummock grass' that covers more than 20 per cent of Australia, and is found in low-nutrient soils of the sand plains and the rocky low mountain ranges in the arid inland and along the coast. It's also called 'porcupine' grass, which gives an indication of how difficult it was to negotiate; in fact, Stuart's horses and his men suffered from often serious injuries caused by the pricking, scratching and ripping of this grass.

He carried on along the edge of the Great Victoria Desert, which runs along the southern central Australian plains, eventually hitting Miller's Water (near what is now Ceduna) before returning to civilisation.

While this expedition made Stuart's reputation, and supplied the government with his invaluable maps and diaries, he received little more than a gold watch from the Royal Geographical Society. Clearly, money and fame were not driving motivations. He was anxious to set out again, perhaps, as Rick Moore explained, because he was a man with personal goals and once he'd set his sights on his long-term mission of crossing the entire continent through its centre, he was determined to continue.

Stuart applied for a pastoral lease at Chambers Creek, and offered to survey the area himself. In April 1859, he set off with a party of three men and fourteen horses, completing the survey of his own land, which he was entitled to lease as its discoverer, and then moving northwards. He was determined to reach the border between Southern Australia and what is now known as the Northern Territory – once again, inhospitable land that had defeated many prospectors and explorers before him.

Stuart preferred to travel in rocky 'Gibber Country', (gibber is an Australian term for a rock or stone) where there is more chance of finding water. In sand dunes, the water disappears underground or evaporates into the air. However, travelling across rocky ground meant he wore out a lot of horseshoes. He was better prepared this time, with ample water and rations, but he was forced to turn back just 100 kilometres short of the border because they had run out of horseshoes.

There were, however, important discoveries en route. In particular he found another water supply, a 'beautiful

Previous pages and right: *Desert landscapes in the area around the mound springs, near the border between Southern Australia and the Northern Territory.*

spring' fed by what we now know is the Great Artesian Basin. He wrote: 'I have named this "The Spring of Hope". It is a little brackish, not from salt, but soda, and runs a good stream of water. I have lived upon far worse water than this: to me it is of the utmost importance, and keeps my retreat open. I can go from here to Adelaide any time of the year and in any sort of season.' He returned in July with reports of 'wonderful country' – a tribute to his optimism given that this is land barely able to support a few livestock.

McDouall Stuart's third expedition was undertaken, at the outset, for personal reasons. He discovered that in his absence, his Chambers Creek leasehold had been explored and claimed by others after his first expedition, and he was forced to return there to resurvey his claim. Setting out in August 1859, he sorted out his own land and organised other claims for his sponsors, moving on to explore the area west of Lake Eyre, in the Strzelecki Desert, named after the Polish explorer Pawel Edmund Strzelecki. He discovered more artesian springs (see pages 211-216), but in the torrid heat of summer, he began to experience serious problems with his eyes, and had trouble with an increasingly rebellious crew of men. After being forced to endure half rations for long periods, all but one of his men refused to go any further, and Stuart immediately sent them home. His remaining companion, William Kekwick, was dispatched south for provisions and more men, returning with thirteen horses, rations for three months, but only a single willing man – Benjamin Head. Kekwick was a loyal companion to McDouall Stuart, and would remain with him to the end of his career, organizing supply bases while Stuart scouted the surrounding areas.

Political change was afoot in Australia during this time, and exploration 'fever' was widespread. Britain had become an acknowledged leader in world exploration, and the empty, uncharted and blank depths of Australia's interior were becoming something of an embarrassment to the Crown. Communication with the continent was also slow and unreliable, and after the invention of the telegraph (Samuel Morse sent his first message in 1844), there was a desire to find a way to extend this technology across the country to the populated south. The line from Britain had already reached India, and a number of Australian colonies were competing to host its terminus. Several options were put forward, including running long undersea cables around the continent; however, it seemed to make sense to run the cable undersea only as far as Australia's northern tip, and then run it overland for 3,000 kilometres south to Adelaide. This was not an easy option, as great tracts of the continent's interior had yet to be charted, and its remoteness and wild unknowns made crossing it a daunting prospect. The Southern Australian government offered a reward of £2,000 for anyone who could find a suitable route for the telegraph, and Chambers and Finke asked the government to put up £1,000 to equip an expedition led by Stuart. Instead, however, it put its faith in explorer Alexander Tolmer, whose expedition failed when he was unable to travel any further than the settled districts of the southern continent.

If Stuart was offended by this slight, given his growing reputation, it did not stop him from continuing his personal mission to cross the continent, and his fourth expedition began in March 1860, when he, Head and Kekwick set out from Chambers Creek, travelling light, with only a few pack horses. Stuart was becoming increasingly sure that the best way to cross the continent was to carry as little as possible, relying on bush tucker and water sources en route, travelling quickly and avoiding delays and complications at all cost.

Around this time, the government of Victoria had their own plans to find a route across the continent, which would terminate in their state in the south. They decided to compete against the Southern Australian government, by funding a lavish expedition headed by none other than Burke and Wills, whose story was told on pages 36–39. The Victoria government spent almost £12,000 (equivalent to £800,000 today) sponsoring this team, with their unbelievably complicated and extravagant entourage.

Stuart was probably unaware of Burke and Wills' grand plans at this stage, as he pressed on towards the centre of the continent. This was a difficult expedition, with unseasonal rain destroying the majority of their supplies, forcing them to continue on half rations. Water became increasingly hard to find, despite the rains, and scurvy began to set in. Head was a big man, and the half rations made him lose considerable amounts of weight, leaving

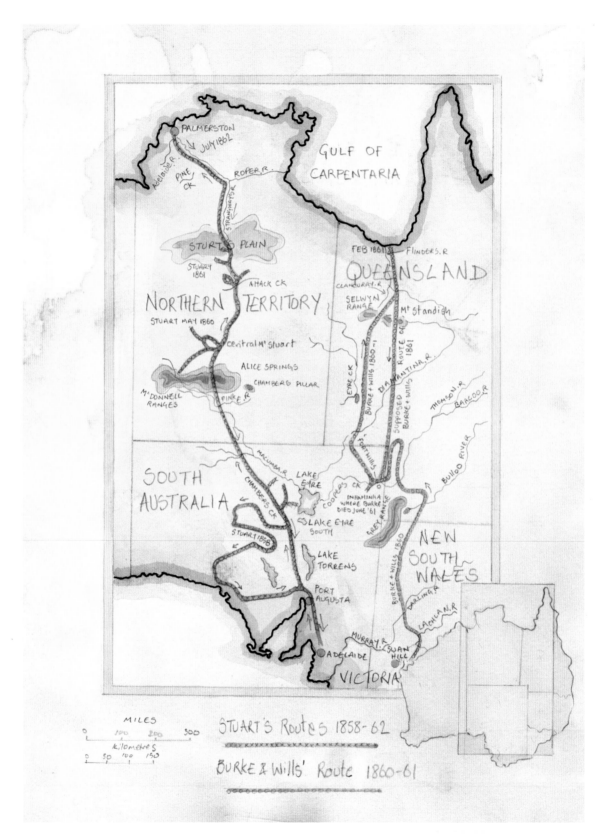

PALMERSTON
JULY 1862
Adelaide R.
PINE CK
ROPER R
STRANGWAYS R

GULF OF
CARPENTARIA

STURT'S PLAIN
STUART 1861

FEB 1861 — Flinders R.

QUEENSLAND

ATTACK CK
CLONCURRY R.
SELWYN RANGE
Mt Standish

NORTHERN TERRITORY
STUART MAY 1860
central Mt Stuart

ROUTE OCT 1861

ALICE SPRINGS
CHAMBERS PILLAR

BURKE + WILLS 1860-1
DIAMANTINA R.

SUPPOSED BURKE + WILLS

McDONNELL RANGES
FINKE R.

EYRE CK
FOOTHILLS

THOMSON R
BARCOO R

BUILOO RIVER

MACUMBA R.
LAKE EYRE

SOUTH AUSTRALIA
CHAMBERS CK

COOPER'S CK
INNAMINKA WHERE BURKE DIED JUNE '61

STUART 1858

LAKE EYRE SOUTH

GREY RANGE

NEW SOUTH WALES

LAKE TORRENS

BURKE + WILLS 1860

PORT AUGUSTA

DARLING R.
LACHLAN R.

MURRAY R.
SWAN HILL

ADELAIDE

VICTORIA

MILES
0   100   200   300
kilometres
0   50   100   150

STUART'S ROUTES 1858-62
xxxxxxxxxxxxxxxxxx

BURKE & WILLS' ROUTE 1860-61

him weak. They eventually found a major water supply in early April, which McDouall Stuart, in tribute to his backer, called Finke River. They followed it over the South Australian border to the MacDonnell Ranges, which he named after Sir Richard Graves MacDonnell, Governor of South Australia.

In the third week of April 1860, Stuart calculated that they had reached the centre of the continent, and he wrote: *'There is a high mount about two miles to the NNE which I hoped would be in the centre but on it tomorrow I will raise a cone of stones and plant the Flag there and will name it Mount Sturt after my excellent and esteemed commander of the expedition in 1844 and 45, Captain Sturt, as a mark of gratitude for the great kindness I received from him during that journey.'*

Below: *You couldn't replicate Stuart's journey today because cattle have overgrazed the land.*

The mountain later became known as Central Mount Stuart, and although it is actually wide of Australia's true centre, this was an important victory for Stuart and his men. And they needed every possible boost, for lack of water forced them to return to camp time after time as they attempted to progress north. Scurvy was becoming debilitating, and only Kekwick was well enough to be capable of heavy work.

Stuart's group headed west into the Tanami Desert, one of the most arid and isolated places on the planet. I know it well because I've travelled there with some aboriginals. Surface water is virtually non-existent and they almost perished. During one of his worst periods Stuart wrote that the muscles of his 'limbs are changing from yellow-green to black'.

In late May, rain allowed them to move northwards more quickly, and in mid-June they reached a river that Stuart named Tennant's Creek. Here they were forced again to change direction, heading north-west into the Tanami again. At one stage the horses went for more than four days without water.

They had travelled thousands of kilometres and were only about 800 kilometres from the northern coast. They'd gone further than anyone before them but progress thereafter was slow, and they were forced to retreat. They came upon another creek, later named 'Attack Creek', but were blocked by dense scrub and hostile aboriginals. Up to that point, Stuart had always had a good relationship with the native peoples, often employing aboriginals in his own expeditions, and was unprepared for the Warramunga people in the north, who raided their camps, threw boomerangs at the horses and set fire to the grass around the camp. Fearing the worst, and with increasingly weak men at his side, Stuart reluctantly decided to turn south.

The return journey to Adelaide was more than 2,400 kilometres, and with weary horses and men – both like walking skeletons – few supplies, and increasingly poor health, it was difficult to proceed. In his typical way, however, Stuart pressed his men on apace, and they returned safely to Chambers Creek in August of 1860, a few days after the massive expedition led by Burke and Wills had left Melbourne.

Although he had been unsuccessful in his ultimate goal, his achievement of crossing the Australian interior finally brought him important recognition. The South Australian government took note, and Stuart's fifth expedition north was undertaken with £2,500 of government money and ten armed men, considered necessary to get past Attack Creek. On the first day of January 1861, Stuart left Chambers Creek with a dozen men, almost 50 horses, and rations for 30 weeks. It was a bad time to be travelling, at the peak of the summer heat, and several men and horses were quickly sent back. The Burke and Wills expedition had reached the Gulf of Carpentaria in mid-February, while Stuart's expedition was still in the north of Southern Australia.

In the MacDonnell Ranges, near Australia's centre, the party came across the footprints they had left a year earlier – indicating that no rain had fallen for that entire period. As luck would have it, it rained the following day and these heavy rains cooled the air and allowed them travel at a faster pace. They reached Attack Creek in late April. At about this time Burke and Wills had returned to their base camp at Cooper's Creek, only to find it deserted. They'd lost Charles Gray by then, and Burke and Wills themselves would die within the next few days, leaving only King to carry on; he was rescued by local aboriginals, but was unable to complete the journey.

Over the next two weeks, Stuart and his party made several attempts to find a route over the plains to the north-west of the country, which were blocked by thick scrub and suffered from a complete dearth of water. Stuart decided, then, to head due north – discovering what he called 'a splendid sheet of water', some 150 metres wide and 7 kilometres in length, which he named Glandfield Lagoon, after the then Mayor of Adelaide, Edward Glandfield. This name was later changed to Newcastle Waters, after a scandal involving the mayor.

The waters provided great respite from their journey, and Stuart and his team camped for almost five weeks, while Stuart and small parties of men scouted around to find a north-western route that would take them to the Victoria River and the sea.

Sturt's Plain is a fierce, hot waterless plain that is really a continuation of the Tanami Desert. The men had no water for many days, even on their retreat. An alternative route north was attempted through a forest of bullwaddi bush, which bushmen describe as nature's attempt to grow barbed wire. Again they failed so they headed north-east towards the Gulf, where they again hit the waterless Sturt's Plain, a forest of low eucalyptus. In all, Stuart and his men attempted to get to the coast eleven times, and simply could not manage it.

In August, Stuart wrote: 'The scrub we were compelled to return from was the thickest I have ever had to contend with. The horses would not face it. They turned about in every direction, and we were in danger of losing them. In two or three yards they were quite out of sight. In the short distance we penetrated it has torn our hands, faces, clothes, and, what is of more consequence, our saddle-bags, all to pieces.'

They suffered more difficulties with the aboriginals, and were forced to set up an armed sentry. Spirits were low, and provisions even lower. Six months after setting out, Stuart admitted defeat and the men were forced to return home, just a few hundred kilometres short of their goal. When they got back, Stuart must have been disheartened to hear of the deaths of all but one of the Burke and Wills party.

Nevertheless, he was keen to continue his expeditions, immediately mounting plans for a sixth, and was also interested in searching for the missing men, but the government was reluctant to fund him. Instead, the people of Adelaide rallied round to provide supplies and offer their services. At the last minute the government stepped in and provided £2,000, on the condition that he took along a scientist. Stuart had failed to find anything of any economic value in his travels, and almost all of the land he came across was unfit for much more than grazing – and even this became impossible during periods of drought. As a result, it was thought that the centre of Australia held little financial promise, and backers and support from the business community and government dwindled in all of Australia's states and territories.

Stuart's sixth and last expedition is the one that has captured the imagination of so many. Despite failing health, and little interest and support, he achieved the unthinkable, and not only managed to traverse the country from top to bottom and back again, something he had nearly achieved several times before, but was also able to clearly map his journeys. It was his work – his precise maps and his journals – that allowed the first telegraph to be built through the centre of Australia, and, of course, made it possible for the men who worked on it to survive in the arid country.

Stuart's sixth expedition departed from Chambers Creek on 8 January 1862 with companions William Darton Kekwick (second officer), Francis William Thring (third officer), William Patrick Auld, Stephen King, John W. Billiatt, James Frew, Heath Nash, John McGorrery and Frederick George Waterhouse, a naturalist. Three were born in Australia, while the others hailed from England. King was the youngest at only nineteen years of age. They took with them 71 horses, so that some could rest while others carried provisions and the men themselves.

His 'official starting' was supposed to have been 25 October of the previous year, when he left the home of his sponsors James and Catherine Chambers in North Adelaide – but it was not the best of starts. Many of his men became so drunk they fell off their horses, and one horse stamped on Stuart's hand, leaving it a bloody mess. He became seriously ill and it was believed that amputation might be required to save his life. He recovered, though his hand was crippled, and a month later set out again with his party.

Things were difficult, as they had, once again, set out in the heat of summer. Eight horses were lost in the first three weeks and many of the provisions had to be left behind. The party was already on starvation rations just one month into the journey. By February 1862 they were in sight of the MacDonnell Ranges – the fifth time Stuart had crossed this territory.

In April, Stuart and his men reached his former camp at Newcastle Waters, where he rested his horses and his men before the difficult passage across Sturt's Plain, which had foiled him on his previous expedition. He made several scouting trips ahead of his men, and eventually discovered a series of waterholes, creeks, springs and rivers, which he named after his companions. It must have felt amazing to come across a ready supply of water, which he had missed during three previous explorations of that territory.

This third attempt to reach the north of the country was in some ways easier than in the past, largely because Stuart had become familiar with the landscape, and adept at finding water when required. He was a confident bushman, and his tracking skills improved with every expedition, as he learned through experience how to 'read' the landscape in order to survive.

The party experienced problems with hostile aboriginals once again, and although Stuart was loathe to do so, he was forced to use firearms to scare them off, or 'warn them'. There are no recorded incidents in which any natives were killed or injured. His journals contain many references to his keen interest in their activities and characteristics; for example, he says he admired the 'bold spirit' of one aboriginal child, as well as the planning and execution of their confrontation at Attack Creek.

From here, travel became much more difficult. Stuart and his scouts tried five times to find a route to the Victoria River without any success. Finally he headed north rather than north-west and was rewarded with a series of small waterholes leading to Daly Waters, about 150 kilometres north of Newcastle Waters. He was, however, faced with the same plains that had defeated him on his previous expeditions, and the thick-thorned scrub seemed to bar further progress. Stuart made one last attempt to reach the Victoria River before continuing north into the Top End. On 9 June he reached territory that had already been mapped and on 1 July he arrived at what he thought was the Adelaide River (in Arnhem Land).

After more trial-and-error expeditions around the edge of what is now Kakadu National Park, they eventually saw the ocean in July. This was the high point of Stuart's life, though his physical and psychological health were fading. He had scurvy and he was nearly blind; even before reaching the northern coast, he had serious doubts that he would make it home to Adelaide. Finally, on 24 July 1862 Stuart reached the beach at Chambers Bay (east of present-day Darwin). He wrote in his diary:

'At eight miles and a half came upon a broad valley of black alluvial soil, covered with long grass; from this I can hear the wash of the sea. On the other side of the valley, which is rather more than a quarter of a mile wide, is growing a line of thick heavy bushes, very dense, showing that to be the

Right: *A replica of the tent Stuart used, erected near Chambers Creek. There were walls that he could attach in bad weather.*

boundary of the beach. Crossed the valley, and entered the scrub, which was a complete network of vines. Stopped the horses to clear a way, whilst I advanced a few yards on to the beach, and was gratified and delighted to behold the water of the Indian Ocean in Van Diemen Gulf [now the Gulf of Carpentaria], before the party with the horses knew anything of its proximity. Thring, who rode in advance of me, called out "The Sea!" which so took them all by surprise, and they were so astonished, that he had to repeat the call before they fully understood what was meant. Then they immediately gave three long and hearty cheers. I dipped my feet, and washed my face and hands in the sea, as I promised the late Governor Sir Richard MacDonnell I would do if I reached it.

He carved his initials – JMDS – on a large tree. The next day, exactly nine months since leaving Adelaide, the Union Jack was raised on the northern shore at Chambers Bay. After only 48 hours at this northern sea Stuart turned towards home. They faced a return journey of 3,400 kilometres along the same route and this journey rates as one of the greatest feats of survival in Australian exploration.

His horses were weak, and many had died or had to be left behind before they entered the Sturt Plains. They struggled again for water, until they reached the MacDonnell Ranges. In the desert many waterholes are temporary, and dry up or are damaged by wildlife. Even Stuart's methodical charting meant that they were unable to find the water that had sustained them on the journey north. Stuart was close to death by now, and his journal contains a vivid record of his sufferings. The years of continual hardship on his many trips, with only brief intervals between, were now taking their toll, and it seems that having finally reached his goal, he lacked the energy or inclination to continue. He was not a glory-seeker, and the prospect of fanfare upon his return would have been unlikely to sustain him. He wrote: 'I am very doubtful of my being able to stand the journey back to Adelaide. Whatever may occur, I must submit to the will of Divine Providence.'

His eyesight failed and Auld took over the recording, taking time to nurse Stuart. In later years, he was moved to tears when he recalled the suffering that Stuart had experienced and it was the compassion of his men that was to save him. When he could no longer ride, McGorrery, the blacksmith, constructed a stretcher mounted between two long poles and Stuart was carried some 960 kilometres between two horses. He made it to Adelaide on 17 December 1862, with all of his men intact, and some 48 of his original horses.

They arrived in a train at Adelaide station to a welcoming crowd. Stuart was a South Australian hero, and his triumph over the tortuous climate and terrain was a spectacular achievement. But his homecoming was marred. He discovered that his great friend and backer, James Chambers, had died the previous August. What's more, Stuart was soon forgotten by the nation once the excitement had died down. He didn't have a home or family, and although he still had his leasehold at Chambers Creek, he was too weak and ill to work the land so he sold it to John Chambers and Alfred Barker.

His right hand remained crippled because of his accident in Adelaide at the outset of his journey, and he was unable to work as a surveyor. There seemed nothing to live for, and he struggled to find his place in urban society when his home for so many years had effectively been the Australian desert. He lacked any real purpose in life. His great friend William Finke offered some comfort and assistance, but Finke tragically died in early 1864, leaving Stuart a broken man. He began to drink heavily, and eventually became something of a social embarrassment, ostracised by the countrymen whose ambitions he had almost single-handedly achieved. He was dismissed as being an inappropriate candidate for a knighthood because of his alcohol problems, and even the £2,000 reward for crossing the country was denied to him.

The Northern Territory was given to South Australia as a dependency, and Stuart was hailed as a legendary figure – but he was friendless and had no money or home. In 1864, he returned to Scotland and when he died in Glasgow two years later only seven people attended his funeral. His sister, Mary Turnbull, arranged for the erection of the tombstone that still marks his grave in Kensal Green cemetery, north London. It was damaged during the Second World War, and the Royal Geographical Society of South Australia arranged its restoration in the early 1980s.

Just three years after his death the government of South Australia established a settlement in Darwin, and in 1870 began to build the telegraph link that would eventually run between Darwin in the north and Adelaide in the south. Stuart's work was complete, and his efforts were crucial in the development of both transportation and communication links that would join Australia to the rest of the world. He also provided maps and charts that allowed the more fertile areas he reached, particularly those around springs and waterholes, to become pastoral land, and the site of settlements. Alice Springs, for example, was established at one of his base camps, and remains one of the largest cities in the Australian outback.

After his death, however, some surveyors and explorers began to question his reputation and achievement. The first surveyors sent to locate the area where he reached the coast failed to locate the tree he had marked or the flag he had erected. Even his companions were unable to find the site of the tree, and although they staunchly defended their leader, they were discredited by the suggestion that their party had not achieved the goal of reaching the northern coast after all. The problem is that longitude is very difficult to establish accurately. Stuart was very good with a compass and notebook but my suspicion is that he just paid lip service to the sextant that was foisted on him by his backers.

Anyway, despite his meticulous approach to charting and mapping his journey, he was out on several points. He had, in the end, followed the Mary and not the Adelaide River to the coast. Half a degree of longitude (approximately 35 miles or 60 kilometres) separated the two rivers. Unbelievably, it took almost 20 years before his tree was located and photographed, with his initials still clearly visible. His name was cleared, and his hero status restored, but it was a sad ending for a man who had achieved so much.

Stuart's achievements laid the foundations for much growth in Australia. As a result of his journeys, the opening up of the Northern Territory was made possible, and a route established for an Overland Telegraph line linking South Australia with India and the rest of the world in 1872. The surveyors who worked on the Overland Telegraph were astonished by the thoroughness of his charts of the route, which extended out 30 to 50 kilometres to either side. It was a classic case, common in exploration, of a little man from a poor background, with no title, who hadn't been to public school, yet who stood up to the establishment.

A settlement was established on the north coast at Darwin and vast areas of the north were opened up for pastoral and mineral development.

The transcontinental highway, which follows almost the exact route of his journeys, still bears his name – the Stuart Highway. Today the trip is infinitely easier, of course. You get a false sense when you travel along it at 100 kilometres an hour on well-maintained roads because of course it was nothing like that for Stuart. The original Central Australia Railway (known as the Ghan), built from Adelaide to Alice Springs, followed a similar route. In 1876 the line started from Port Augusta, and it was extended to Oodnadatta in 1891. In 2004 a rail link across the country was fully established – almost 141 years after Stuart had first carved his initials on that tree in the Northern Territory.

Much may have changed since Stuart laid foot on the Australian interior so many years ago, but this still remains land that is unbelievably difficult, and even now it is hard to believe that a single man and a small crew could have

Above and below: *It was a morning ritual for Stuart to go to a high point and look out for signs of water: green trees, birds such as finches, kangaroos or wallabies.*

journeyed across it with any success. I decided to venture into the desert, but not to retrace Stuart's steps all the way from south to north and back again – it would have taken far too much time even using modern transportation. Instead, I wanted to examine the different ways in which Stuart was able to solve the problem of finding enough water in this bone-dry landscape to keep his crew and horses alive and get them back home again.

We know that water was always an issue for Stuart, and he developed a series of methods for uncovering sources. He had a telescope and, later, binoculars, which allowed him to search the horizon for signs that there may be water in the vicinity. He learned that bird life often denoted a water supply. Even a solitary bird could indicate water nearby; it might be dipping into a pond or spiralling over an area where it knew there was water. Some birds, such as pigeons and finches, are more water-reliant than others and Stuart discerned the ones that were best to watch. Pigeons fly fast towards water and more slowly away from it, but it's not easy to judge speed from the ground.

Often, wildlife led him to water. Footprints and animal tracks were always a good sign, and he learned to look out for kangaroos and rock wallabies, who appeared at night and would often indicate water in the vicinity. In desperation, Stuart could also rely on his horse. There is no better diviner than a thirsty horse, and his diaries indicate that on many occasions, they followed their mounts, sometimes for miles and miles, to a natural water source.

A mist rising from any area of the land – evaporation in the heat from water – was also a sign that there might be a still pond. He studied the contours of the land looking for a dip on the horizon, which might signify water. He also looked for greener, taller plants in the forest or scrubland, which might indicate that they were being fed by a watercourse or spring. Where a reed grew, he knew there would be a permanent source of water, and he learned to spot these from long distances. Aboriginals would look for certain trees, such as paperbark or boab trees, which can store water, or the roots of desert kurrajongs, but there is no record that Stuart picked up this skill.

In some cases, where plants are thriving but there is no immediate source of water, it may be that there is an underground source that can be bored down to. If you push a stick down into the earth and pull it out again, you should be able to judge how moist the soil is and how far down the water table lies. If it looks like a promising source, you dig a hole about 30 centimetres below the depth at which you hit saturated ground. Let it fill with water and bail out the first lot, which will be dirty. Let it refill and settle again and it may be safe to drink. If you want to use the well again, cover the hole with sticks or bark, or a large stone, to prevent animals drinking from it and contaminating it.

While we were in the desert, I demonstrated the transpiration method of getting water, where I attached a polythene bag tightly to a branch of a eucalyptus tree and left it for a day, and I managed to collect more than

Above: *A desalination still. Salty water is boiled over the fire and the steam runs in a tube through a cooling tank. Distilled water flows out into the pan.*

half a litre. You need to choose a leafy branch and make sure you tie the bag on tightly enough to make an airtight seal. Sunlight on the leaves causes condensation to form inside the bag and the water pools at the lowest corner.

It is important, too, to take advantage of any rain that does fall. Anyone in the outback gets used to catching and storing rain whatever way they can, tipping water off any large leaves before it is absorbed, collecting rain in cans and tarpaulins, and filling any empty vessel to hand. Avoid canvas tarpaulins or tents that have been chemically treated, though, and never drink water from the leaves of toxic plants.

To desalinate brackish water, you need to improvise a kind of still. Boil water in a can with a tube attached. The tube should then be run through a cooling tank of salt water so that the steam condenses into desalinated water, which can be collected in a plastic bag or a pan. It's not an ideal solution to a lack of water, though, as you need to distill a lot of salt water to get a decent amount of drinking water.

One of the most astonishing phenomena that Stuart came across was what are now known as the 'mound springs'. The chain of mound springs in the Lake Eyre region of South Australia are a permanent source of water in an otherwise dry, arid interior. John McDouall Stuart must have been amazed and delighted when he first came upon these little hills rising up from the desert with basins of clean, brackish water in the tops.

He wrote: 'They are really remarkable springs – such a height above the level of the plain; I saw them from a hill on Chambers Creek (the Twins). From whence do they derive their supply of water, to cause them to rise to such a height? It must be from some high ranges to the north-west, or a large body of fresh water lying on elevated ground. This is another strange feature of the mysterious interior of Australia.'

I talked to Colin Harris, President of an organisation called Friends of the Mound Springs, who explained to me how they are formed. The water in the mound springs in the heart of the Australian desert enters the Great Artesian Basin (one of the largest artesian groundwater basins in the world) on the western slopes of the Great Dividing Range in Queensland, where there is permeable sandstone at the surface. Smaller quantities of water are also

thought to enter from the Western Desert in the south-east region of the Northern Territory. This water moves under the continent at a very slow rate of 1 to 3 metres a year, meaning that it can take up to 1.5 to 2 million years to travel from the recharge areas in eastern Queensland to the discharge areas around Lake Eyre in South Australia. This means it's really a kind of fossil water.

As it moves underground through water-bearing sands and sandstones it dissolves a lot of solids along the way, so by the time it gets to the edge of the basin, it is full of minerals, sulphides, chlorates and other salts. As the water emerges at the surface, these salts precipitate out and form cones that are sometimes metres and metres in height and look like volcanos. These are the distinctive 'mounds'.

The water from mound springs is brackish but it is fine to drink. Certainly, it would have quenched the thirst of Stuart's horses and they must have been delighted to come across it. I tried some and while it's probably not up to World Health Organisation standards for drinking water, it's perfectly potable. For Stuart, these mound springs were the key to his success – the way he got through the harshest bit of desert with the lowest rainfall and reached the tropical lands to the north.

Due to their isolation in the desert over many millennia, mound springs have developed a unique ecology with many rare and endangered species of flora and fauna. Some individual springs or clusters of springs have species that have developed or adapted to thrive in their specific location. This is a godsend to anthropologists, who can study first-hand how species adapt to certain climates and conditions.

Most springs have a luxuriant growth of sedges that help to stabilise the sediment and provide shelter for the animals. Reeds and grasses, green algae, Cyanobacteria, salt-tolerant species such as the succulent samphire and a rare, endemic species of button grass grow in or around the springs. Invertebrates found in the springs include small crustaceans such as phreatocid isopods, amphipods, prawns and ostracods, which are sometimes endemic to one group of springs. Fish, such as desert gobies, are also common in many mound springs. Some of these species, such as the salt pipewort (button grass), numerous snails and crustacea, and the dalhousie goby (fish), are

Above: *An old mound spring that Reg Dodd showed me, which is used as a table at male initiation ceremonies.*

Pages 212-213: *Blanche Cup mound spring.*

unique to a particular spring and thus prone to extinction if the springs are not managed carefully.

Unfortunately, from the 1860s onwards, bores driven along stock routes, transportation and communication passages, and mineral, gas and oil exploration, have meant that the flow of water is now less pressurised, and therefore the springs do not receive as much water, year on year.

Many springs have also disappeared in the last 100 years as a result of water extraction from the Great Artesian Basin, probably resulting in the extinction of some unique species before they were even discovered.

Thankfully, in the early 1970s, the State Environmental Department realised that activity around these centres, and the increasing demand for water in the arid interior, as well as tourist activity and grazing, meant that mound springs had become fragile, and this was a cause for concern. Since that time, most have been protected and the land around them is carefully monitored to prevent further damage. Several have been fenced in to prevent wildlife (or people) damaging them.

We don't know whether John McDouall Stuart caught fish in the mound springs to cook and eat, but we do know that he and his men took a gadget for lighting fires on their expeditions. The John McDouall Stuart Museum in Adelaide displays an interesting item that looks somewhat like a miniature cannon. It has a flint and steel and a hollow tube attached. I was intrigued by this mechanism, and in my shed at home I managed to recreate one.

I realised that they must have used some sort of cord in the interior of the barrel, so that a spark could ignite it, and it could then be used to light some dry grass or a piece of dung. I couldn't find steel nickel like the original, but I fashioned my model out of brass, using a cord impregnated with saltpetre in the barrel, which was enormously effective. The cord is easily extinguished after use if you put your thumb over the end of the barrel. Stuart may also have used a mirror or a magnifying glass to create heat over dry brush, which would start a fire almost instantly in the heat of the day.

As the primary source of water for the interior of Australia, the springs were important centres for aboriginal communities. This is demonstrated by the large abundance of stone chips, grinding stones and other artefacts in their vicinity. All springs in desert country are sacred sites for the Arabanna tribe and other peoples, and were important for many traditional ceremonies and as part of their native song cycles. Sadly, John McDouall

Above: *The fire-lighting kit taken on Stuart's travels in the desert. The hollow tube (bottom) would have contained some kind of cord, and the flint and steel (above) would have sparked to ignite it.*

Right: *Grindstone quarries are evidence that aboriginal people inhabited this area.*

Stuart played an unwitting part in the destruction of some of these places by mapping them. Men working on the construction of the Overland Telegraph relied on his maps, in which he charted water sources, and many became overused, leading them to dry up or become tainted by human pollution and that of their animals.

I talked to an old aboriginal man called Reg Dodd who explained to me about the clash of cultures that occurred after Stuart opened up the interior. He took me to the site of a stone table that was thousands of years old, where they used to hold ceremonies in which boys became men, eat ceremonial dinners and various other activities. In 1871, a railway line was built going right past it, meaning there was no privacy for them to hold ceremonies there any more.

Mining corporations came along prospecting for gems and minerals, ranchers brought cattle and sheep to graze and, in the worst development of all for aboriginal people, Australian government agencies working in conjunction with Christian church missions began a policy of taking aboriginal children away from their families. It is estimated that this policy, which continued from about 1869 until 1969, was responsible for the removal of 100,000 children to internment camps, orphanages and other institutions in an attempt to raise them to think and act like white people. The people behind this policy genuinely believed they were doing the children a favour by introducing them to a Western diet, lifestyle, religion and manners, but their actions were responsible for the dying out of a lot of traditional aboriginal wisdom about medicine and survival in the outback.

In aboriginal culture, knowledge is passed from generation to generation and when the children were removed, there was no one to pass the stories on to. Traditionally, things were learned at different ages. An elderly female relative might teach you one thing and your grandfather might show you another. This was wisdom that could not be taught in a classroom. You would be taken out into the bush to see the features of the land and shown: 'That hill is a bearded dragon, or a goanna, and a snake came out of that spring.' Reg compared the removal of the children and the introduction of mining to the outback to tearing pages out of a book. Some knowledge can no longer be passed on, he says, because too many pages have been lost.

Above: *Stuart's charts opened up the country to cattlemen, who were soon overgrazing the land.*

If you want to learn more about the so-called 'stolen generations', the 2002 Australian film *Rabbit-Proof Fence*, based on the book *Follow the Rabbit-Proof Fence* by Doris Pilkington Garimara, is a good introduction. It tells of the author's mother and two other young mixed-race aboriginal girls who ran away from Moore River Native Settlement, north of Perth, in which they were placed in 1931, in order to return to their aboriginal families. In interviews, Doris told her own story: she was taken away from her mother at the age of three or four and told that her mother had given her away. They were not reunited until she was 25 and, by that time, Doris was unable to speak her native language and had been taught to regard indigenous culture as evil.

As well as children, elderly people were removed to live out their years in care homes. This stripped the middle generations of both their historical links to the past, traditionally passed on by tribe elders, as well as their future. Aboriginal people have a complex system

Above: *The grave of Mary Hewish, right in the middle of the desert. A King Brown slithered into her bed and bit her and they tried to get a doctor to come out but the location was just too remote.*

of family relations, where each person knows their kin and their land. Kinship systems define where a person fits in to the community, binding people together in relationships of sharing and obligation. These systems may vary across communities but they serve similar functions across Australia. Elders bridge the past and the present and provide guidance for the future. They teach important traditions and pass on their skills, knowledge and personal experiences. It is for these reasons that in indigenous societies elders are treated with respect.

One of the crucial things that aboriginal elders encouraged was a love and maintenance of the land upon which they lived. They carefully maintained waterholes and sacred sites to allow them to flourish, and to ensure that the Dreaming continued, that aboriginals could carry on with thousands of centuries of tradition. When the old people were removed to care homes, much of this wisdom and knowledge, including the paths and songs that would allow survival in the desert, died with them.

Reg showed me a waterhole, discreetly covered by rocks, that still remains to this day. The water was sweet and pure, quite different to the brackish water I'd come across in other waterholes in the desert, including those thrown up by the artesian bay springs. He explained that he always cleaned it when he came there, and covered it up with rocks again so that no algae and plantlife could clog it up and the sun wouldn't evaporate it. Unfortunately, many other traditional waterholes the length and breadth of the land haven't been looked after quite so assiduously and they are now unuseable by thirsty travellers.

Today, many of Australia's inland waterways are named after Stuart and his travelling companions, friends and sponsors, as well as government figures, who were prestigious at the time, who he decided to honour. As we travelled across the desert in his footsteps in our 4x4s with satellite phones, GPS navigational systems and plentiful supplies of food and water, my thoughts kept returning to Stuart and marvelling about how he managed to survive in such hostile land. The heat is ferocious and it seldom rains. You are plagued by sandflies and mosquitoes, and we know the same was true for Stuart as one of his men wrote: 'The mosquitoes at this camp have been most annoying; scarcely one of us has been able to close his eyes in sleep during the whole night: I never found them so bad anywhere – night and day they are at us.'

Stuart would have had no way of making contact, other than sending messages when he happened to reach a cattle station – and there weren't any beyond the site of modern-day Alice Springs. When supplies ran low, he may have been able to trap some of the local wildlife – Stuart and his men probably saw kangaroos, desert rats, and various fish, amphibian and lizard life – but they would never have been plentiful enough to meet the needs of his entourage. And water, of course, was an ongoing problem. He probably felt thirsty most of the time.

Today, the desert has various means of transportation criss-crossing its interior, many of them still following Stuart's trails. Even though more is now known about the climate, geology and geography of this great continent, much of it still remains an enigma, and a source of much interest. Back in the mid-19th century, Stuart would have been on his own entirely, documenting

sightings of many flora, fauna and landmarks for the very first time.

This is land that has, after more than a century, been unclaimed and unsettled, even by indigenous populations or livestock. It is very harsh and probably represents one of the most extreme challenges in terms of survival that any man could ever imagine. And yet Stuart, with few resources, and a handful of men he called his 'companions', managed the near impossible. Like Gaston Grady, did he have a particularly strong will to live, or a driving determination that set him apart from his peers? Was he in search of a personal goal, or was he really just at home in the harsh Australian interior? We may never understand his motivation, but we can certainly salute his vision and his achievement.

Left: *Reg Dodds at his aboriginal well. It is his responsibility to maintain it, keeping it clean and replacing the rocks on top so it doesn't dry out in the heat of the sun.*

Below: *Even with the best 4x4's in the world, desert travel is not easy. If you're thinking of copying us, be warned!*

Around the
Torres Strait
Islands

While natives of the Australian mainland are known as aboriginals, those living in the islands of the Torres Strait claim their own identity, and represent a unique collection of cultures that differ enormously from their mainland cousins. The Torres Strait Islands lie in the gap between the northern tip of Cape York and the southern New Guinea mainland, which is only a short distance away. Their inhabitants remain one of the most specialised marine cultures in the world, with a rich, dramatic history, and their pride, dignity and warrior ethos have carved them an important role in Australian heritage.

Left: *Flying around the coast of Prince of Wales Island.*

Roughly 274 islands form the Torres Strait Islands, some of which still remain uncharted. They look like stepping stones between Papua New Guinea and the remote, northern tip of Australia's Cape York Peninsula and remain a traditional link between the Australian mainland and its northern Asian neighbours.

The islands were claimed by Queensland, a constituent State of the Commonwealth of Australia, between 1872 and 1879, to prevent rival colonial powers controlling this increasingly important shipping route and the lucrative pearling industries of the area.

The Torres Strait was once a land bridge that connected present-day Australia with New Guinea in a single land mass known as 'Sahul' or Australia-New Guinea. About 12,000 years ago, this land bridge was submerged by rising sea levels, forming the strait that connects the Arafura and Coral seas. Some of the Torres Strait Islands are part of the northernmost extent of the Great Dividing Range, the extensive series of mountain ranges that runs along almost the entire eastern coastline of Australia.

The islands can be broadly grouped by their geological features and location in the Torres Strait. The Eastern group is volcanic in origin, and comprised mainly of lava and volcanic ash. The Central group are low, sandy islands, some of which are sandbanks that were built up on coral reefs by wind and waves. The High Western group is made of old volcanic and granite rock, while the North Western Low group was created when alluvial mud overlaid old coral reefs.

The islands are also grouped into clusters, which vary considerably depending on which sources and maps you consult. The Eastern Islands are usually considered to include Mer (Murray), Erub (Darnley), Ugar (Stephen), Damut, Waier and Bramble Cay. The lower Western Islands are comprised of Moa (including Kubin and St Paul's communities), Badu and Mabuiag. The top Western group is made up of Saibai, Boigu and Dauan islands, while the Central Islands are Iama (Yam), Warraber (Sue), Poruma (Coconut), Masig (Yorke) and Nagir. Waibene (Thursday), Kirriri (Hammond), Ngurapai (Horn), Goods, Zuna, Tuesday, Wednesday, Friday and Muralug (Prince of Wales) form the Inner Island group, while Sisia, New Mapoon, Bamaga, Umagico and Injinoo are found in the Northern Peninsula Area (NPA).

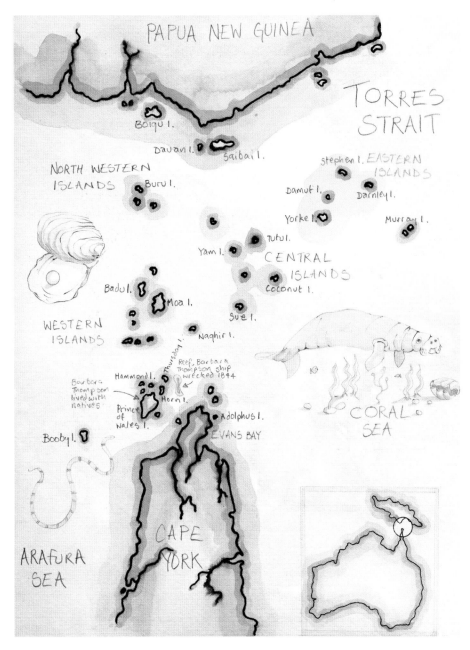

Torres Strait Islanders are Melanesians. 'Melanesia' is the term for a group of islands in the South Pacific Ocean, lying north-east of Australia and south of the Equator, and including New Guinea, the Admiralty Islands, the Bismarck and Louisiade archipelagos, the Solomon Islands, the Santa Cruz Islands, New Caledonia and the Loyalty Islands, Vanuatu, Fiji, Norfolk Island, and numerous others. The islanders are, culturally, most like the coastal peoples of Papua New Guinea. They are therefore

229

regarded as being distinct from other aboriginal peoples of Australia, and are generally referred to separately. An exception is the Kaurareg people of Muralug (Prince of Wales) Island, Hammond and Horn Island who share certain cultural traits and identify with the aboriginal groups of nearby Cape York. Many thousands of Islanders live in Queensland, where they form a strong community, mainly in two areas on the coast – Bamaga and Seisia.

The first inhabitants of the Torres Strait probably migrated from the Indonesian archipelago about 70,000 years ago, when New Guinea was still attached to the Australian mainland. New waves of migration followed, including some from the Australian continent itself.

Although it is likely that Chinese, Malay and Indonesian traders had explored the islands before him, the first navigator credited with coming across the islands is the Spaniard Luis Vaez de Torres who sailed through the strait in 1606, while searching for the 'southern continent'.

The original inhabitants lived in small communities, relying on fishing, hunting and the growing of crops for their subsistence. This is interesting, because aboriginal populations on the Australian mainland did not often cultivate food; instead, they hunted and collected (making them hunter-gatherers), fished and set traps. Aboriginal peoples ate a large variety of foods in a systematic and sustainable manner, using gathering techniques that ensured no one food source was over-exploited. They ate wild fruit, nuts, berries, edible leaves and plant roots, but always made sure that enough seeds were left so that new growth could take place. The young of any animal species, or any female still caring for its offspring, were rarely killed. When collecting eggs, some were always left to hatch thus ensuring the survival of the species.

In the islands, however, and particularly those in the

Right: *Shellfish was a staple of the Torres Islanders' diet, and the shells were used to make jewellery and a variety of decorative and functional items.*

northern areas, their practices were similar to those of the New Guinea mainland. Using 'swidden' techniques, which involve burning back vegetation and leaving the land fallow for several years to ensure its fertility, they cultivated yams, taros, and a variety of other root crops, as well as bananas. Early settlers and explorers spoke of the islanders' 'gardens'. Over the years, foreigners introduced new varieties to the plants already grown, and new crops such as corn and sweet potato, which could be readily absorbed into local agriculture and brought a greater diversity to their diet. These staple foods were supplemented by coconuts, and other fruit- and nut-bearing trees. The plentiful marine life provided a huge variety of fish, shellfish and turtles, as well as sea birds and eels.

On some of the islands, it is difficult to find fresh water during the dry season because the run-off from the hills is fast and the acidic soils do not absorb much water, except in rocky basins. Today, there are reservoirs for water on inhabited islands, which hold enough for the populations. Despite water shortages, there is abundant plant and wildlife, and many of the plants in the islands were prized for their ability to provide moisture when sucked and chewed.

The climate in the Torres Strait region is largely tropical, with November being the hottest month, January the wettest, and July the coldest, although there is only a few degrees change in temperature between summer and winter. During the wet seasons, north-west monsoons sweep down from Asia and cyclones are prevalent. In recent years flooding has become a serious problem. Low-lying areas have always been prone to floods each year when high tides combine with north-west winds; however, these floods are now becoming more severe (thought to be the result of climate change associated with global warming) and some important cultural sites have been inundated.

The Torres Strait hosts its own 'bioregion', characterised by extensive shoals, banks and up to 27 species of mangroves. These are a diverse group of predominantly tropical shrubs and trees that have an amazing array of roles. Mangroves protect the coast from erosion and provide a habitat for wildlife such as birds and crocodiles, as well as snakes, spiders, numerous insects, amphibians and, of course, other plants. They also provide food, shelter and breeding areas for fish and crustaceans, including prawns, mud and blue swimmer crabs, barramundi, whiting, flathead, bream and mullet. Biologists estimate that 75 per cent of the commercially caught fish and prawns in the Queensland area spend at least some part of their life cycle in the mangroves. For many species of fish, like sea mullet and barramundi, the muddy waters of the mangroves are the nurseries where they raise their young.

Mangroves survive in silty soils in waterways that are salty with little available oxygen, conditions in which most other plants would die. One of the most interesting features of the mangrove is the slim aerial roots called pneumatophores that surround the maturing plants like a small forest. These can grow up to heights of 20 centimetres from the surface of the mud. They act as supports for the plants and are an extension of the mass of intertwining underground roots. Mangroves have the amazing ability to breathe in oxygen through these aerial roots when they are exposed at low tide. The roots in the mud have a filter-like structure that removes most of the salt in the water as they suck it up to the leaves. Mangroves have evolved salt pores to extrude salt. These actively push the salt out of the plant to maintain as low a salt/water ratio as possible inside the mangrove itself. If you run your finger along the leaves, you'll see a white, powdery substance – salt! Leaves release carbon dioxide and oxygen, but in most land trees, water evaporates during the process. Because they have thick and waxy leaves, less water evaporates from mangroves in the hot sun of the day. This again helps the mangrove to conserve what fresh water it has and minimises the need to take up sea water through its roots.

Many travellers and explorers preferred to steer clear of the mangrove swamps, probably because they look so inhospitable, and are hard to negotiate because of the tangle of roots; the flowers of most mangrove trees are not pleasant, the brackish water smells typically swamplike, and there is, of course, always a fear of crocodiles. However, when the tide goes out, mangrove swamps provide a feast of bush food.

We experienced some of the bounty first hand, with two Islanders as

guides. We set out in the mangroves to find mud mussels, which are known to the Islanders as 'uckles'. When the first mussel was found, Enid, a junior elder of the Kaurareg people, broke it open and cast it to the four directions, asking her ancestors to make the mud that contained good mussels come to the surface, and mud that contained empty shells to go underground so that we would be successful in our foraging – which we were. Like mainland aboriginals, the Islanders have very strong bonds with their land – a spiritual engagement – and they take care to thank their ancestors for nature's bounty, and to ask for wildlife, plants, and everything on earth to remain fertile.

Ilana, a native mangrove comber, showed me how to locate depressions in the mud then burrow down to find mud mussels, which are like large versions of the mussels we are familiar with in the UK. She cooked them over a fire on the beach.

The traditional kind of Torres Island beach barbecue, known as an 'ami' is made of hot rocks. Here's a description of an ami from the journals of a seaman called Oswald Brierly, written between 1840 and 1850: *'Stones are spread over the bottom of it, shallow with sloping sides, and upon this a fire is made and a number of stones put into it. When the stones are thoroughly heated, the fire is taken out from amongst them, the heated stones being left in the pit. The sloping sides of the pit are now lined with the bark of the tea-tree which is laid all round against the sand. Over the bottom of the pit they lay some of the strong coarse grass, not very dry grass, but moderately so. The amis will vary in size. [Women place the food to be cooked inside – yam, turtle, fruits, seafood.] The whole is then covered up with tea-tree bark and sand heaped up above it.'*

Left: *Mud mussels are one of the many foods to be found in a mangrove swamp. It's like a supermarket in there, with plenty of variety.*

Mangrove pods were collected and eaten during the rainy season, when food was scarce. The pods take a great deal of preparation; they are roasted in a hot ami first, then the insides (seeds and fruit) are scraped out and soaked to remove the bitter flavour and carefully washed and squeezed into lumps for eating.

Mangrove worms, known as shipworms (actually bivalve shellfish), are found in holes in old mangrove wood. They are either eaten raw or cooked, depending upon the species. They are also a prized medicine for curing colds and stomach ache. In places, these worms were farmed; logs were pulled into the water and revisited for the harvest a year later. I've eaten and enjoyed them: they taste like crab pâté with a hint of chilli!

During the monsoon season, before the days of supermarkets with air-freighted food, Islanders used to rely heavily on mangrove pods and several types of wild beans, including the Queensland matchbox bean. This indigenous plant is a typical bean vine; the seeds are toxic, but the beans inside can be processed to provide food. This took a great deal of work, much like preparing the mangrove pods, but it was necessary in times when food was scarce. The Torres Strait is one of the few places in the world where this plant is used for food.

The rainy season affected all the islands, of course, but the elders on each one knew intimately which islands had yams, turtle eggs, or flowering and fruiting plants at various times of year – knowledge that was crucial to their survival.

It's unlikely that the flora and fauna of these regions has

Above: *The remains of an ami on Prince of Wales Island. Crab and mud mussels are placed on hot rocks, covered with paperbark and steamed.*

Above: *Enid prepares a 'kup mari', a traditional cooking method used for feasts. First she wraps some pork in coconut fronds to make a neat package. This is placed on top of some hot rocks, along with vegetables in tin foil, then branches and matting are laid on top. When it's opened two to three hours later, the meat is perfectly cooked. We had trouble filming this, because it was in the midst of a tropical storm.*

changed dramatically over the centuries. We found many of the same plants and animals that were mentioned in the diaries of early explorers. We saw hibiscus, Pandanus, which produces a globe-like fruit that is often edible, and coconut. In some of the islands coconuts are not indigenous, and groves have been cultivated. Wongai fruit, also known as the Torres Strait plum, proliferated, and remains an important fruit for the Islanders. They say that if you eat these plums, you will one day come back to the Torres Straits – so I made sure I tried some.

The peanut tree has clusters of large, leathery, boat-shaped pods that turn bright orange-red when ripe to expose large, satiny, blue-black, edible seeds. These are eaten raw or roasted, and taste like peanuts. Custard apple trees are large and spreading, shaded by green drooping leaves. They have light yellow, trumpet-shaped flowers that produce a pungent, sweet smell, especially in the late afternoon when the male pollen sacks burst open. The ripe fruit is soft, white and very moist.

The lady apple tree produces fruit that is deep red and heavily ribbed, with a sharp flavour and crunchy flesh. We also found mangoes and cashew fruit, which were in plentiful supply.

Widespread on the floor of the forests, pepper tree is a shrub that grows to 3 metres tall and produces elongated, conical, fleshy orange fruit when ripe. These are edible, with small, spicy seeds. Early settlers described it as an 'excellent preserve', and noted that if 'gathered green it is equally good pickled'.

The woody climber 'Devils Guts' earns its name from the sharp curved thorns on the stem, which can easily tear the flesh of hapless travellers. It has a large white flower in the spring and summer made conspicuous by tufts of long white stamens.

The majority of the Islanders' time was spent preparing, planting and harvesting all their crops. This was especially so on Murray Island, as it had fertile soil and sufficient rain. Men would prepare the area by cutting down trees and burning the undergrowth. The women would then till the soil. In the western and northern islands, where crops grew poorly, greater emphasis was placed on fruit gathering, collecting shellfish and fishing. Hunting dugong and turtle was important throughout the Torres Strait and still is today (see

Above: *Sam cooking in a termite mound oven. He made a hole in the mound, lit a fire in it, let it heat up then raked the coals and placed a fish inside. This is a traditional cooking method from Papua New Guinea.*

pages 244-247). Islanders also snared and netted birds such as herons, terns and the Torres Strait pigeon. Sea birds and their eggs were taken, as were pied imperial pigeons. The adult pigeons were ambushed with sticks while they flew from the mainlands to island roosts by the same route each evening. Some Islanders built fires under the birds' roosting trees during the day and lit them once the birds had settled, so that the smoke suffocated them. They could then cull the eggs and chicks from the nests and capture the disorientated adults.

Trees were plentiful, and important to the Islanders. They were used to manufacture the large dugout canoes with double outriggers that were in use at the time of European settlement. Large canoes, up to 20 metres long and capable of holding up to 50 people, were obtained through trade with New Guinea and used around the Torres Strait and northern Cape York. Smaller double outriggers were probably made locally. Bark canoes were made of several sheets of bark sewn together with vines.

Bark was a particularly crucial commodity to the Islanders. The most important tree was the paperbark tree, or melaleuca. The larger species of this tree are known as paperbarks, and the smaller types as honey myrtles. One well-known type of melaleuca, the Ti tree (tea tree), *Melaleuca alternifolia*, is notable for its anti-fungal and antibiotic oil, which was traditionally used in indigenous communities and is now sold worldwide. Aboriginals and Islanders used the leaves for a variety of medicinal purposes, for example chewing the young leaves to alleviate headaches. The softness and flexibility of paperbark made it an extremely useful material. It was

Top left: *Two cashew fruits. The yellow fruit is delicious but the green cashew nuts below have to be dehusked and heat-treated to get rid of the prussic acid content before they are edible.*

Bottom left: *When lit, the banksia fruit burns like a slow-burning match.*

Left: *The custard apple is a lovely tropical fruit found throughout the islands.*

used to line coolamons (a traditional, shallow, canoe-shaped dish or vessel with many purposes). It could make cradles or sleeping mats; it was used for wrapping food for cooking (in the same way aluminium foil is used today), as a disposable raincoat, and for tamping holes in canoes. It could also be used to make a temporary shelter, known as a humpie, in wet weather. Large sheets of paperbark were bent over a branch supported by two upright fork-ended branches at either end. The ends were buried in sand and flaps were bent around to cover the opening in bad weather. Paperbark shelters were waterproof and almost mosquito-proof.

It was the men's job to cut large sheets of bark while women stripped smaller pieces. Paperbark was only collected during and just after the wet season when it was pliable and there was plenty of sap in the trees. Stripping paperbark did not harm the tree as a thin layer of bark was left and the same tree could be stripped again in a year or two.

Casuarina trees (also known as 'she-oak' or 'sheoak'), are particularly interesting, and their presence is said to indicate a source of fresh water. In the past, mariners used to look for these trees on the coastline and dig beneath or near them to find a source of water. She-oak was popularly used for making spears. The inner bark and sapwood shavings were soaked in water and the liquid gargled to cure toothache. Indigenous tribes dumped she-oak trunks into rivers or creeks to attract grubs. These were harvested and eaten raw or cooked. Young she-oak cones were chewed to produce saliva in dry mouths, which was useful when travelling long distances in the hot seasons.

The red kurrajong tree (also known as flame kurrajong, or illawarra) was another tree with many uses. Its bark was

Above: *Enid peeling paperbark, traditionally a man's job. There wasn't much on Prince of Wales Island but we found a decent supply at Evans Bay.*

Right: *Traditional shelters were made using a hoop of pandanus branches, bound with bark, and with a paperbark roof on top.*

Page 245: *Turtle tracks on the beach, where a turtle has come out of the sea to lay her eggs. Locals prod the sand with a metal probe and if it comes out with egg yolk on it they dig down and recover the eggs. However, there were no eggs here; I could tell by the tracks that a goanna had beaten us to it.*

soaked in water and thin strips were rolled to produce a kind of string. This string was sometimes woven into string bags for holding food and it was also used as fishing line. Kurrajong bark could also be used to make a flattened sheet for carrying babies in. Waterproof coolamons were made from damp bark, tied at each end with strips of lawyer vine, filled with sand and left to dry; and long wide strips of stringy bark were used to make canoes in the days before wooden canoes became popular. The strip was bent lengthways and the ends stitched together using needles made of lawyer cane stems. Putty made from the bark of the wild peach was used to waterproof the stitches. The sides of the canoe were held outwards by tying branches across the sides and across the bottom. The seeds of the red kurrajongs were also roasted and ground to produce flour, so it was an all-round useful tree.

Traditionally, Torres Strait Islanders have always caught a wide range of marine species for subsistence and cultural uses, and their consumption of seafood remains one of the highest in the world. Among the species they eat are tropical rock lobster, dugong, turtle, shark, fish, crabs and octopus. Their methods include handlining, diving, spearing, reef-gleaning, cast-netting, gill-netting, trolling from dinghies, jigging and seining.

Canoes were used for deep-water fishing, but in certain seasons shoals of small fish lay just off the beaches, where they could be caught with scoops or spears. These 'sardines' also attracted larger fish, which could be caught with spear or line. During the monsoon, when plant foods were in short supply and other kinds of fishing were difficult, the people resorted to large stone fish traps.

Turtles are an important traditional food for aboriginal people and Torres Strait Islanders, and are still caught despite the fact that marine turtles are a protected species. Every part of the turtle is used, including the shell. In 1606, Spanish explorers in the Torres Strait found turtle shell crafted into fish hooks, needles, awls, spoons, combs, masks and ornaments. In the past they were usually hunted with a spear, from a canoe, and today they use a tinny (tin boat) or dingy.

Sometimes, tethered remora (fish which attach themselves to turtles with suckers on their heads) were used in hunting. Twine was attached around the tail, and the remora was lowered into the water near a turtle. If it attached, both remora and turtle could be reeled in together. Around November and December turtles could be captured on sandbanks as they climbed up to lay their eggs. They also used the beaches of the Murray group to lay eggs, and they could be caught there simply by rolling them onto their backs.

Turtle eggs were a prized source of nutrition and were eaten raw or cooked (the white does not become hard with cooking). They could also be used to quench thirst. Islanders had to fight to get to these eggs before other wildlife did. On our travels we found a beach with turtle tracks from a female who had come onshore and laid her eggs before returning to the sea. However, we could see from another set of tracks that a goanna had beaten us to the eggs, and it had left nothing but their leathery cases behind. Many other predators keep an eye out for turtle eggs and, if they manage to hatch, the baby turtles who emerge and make their way to the shore. Some 150 eggs are laid in each nest, but only one or two turtles from every batch will make it through to adulthood.

Dugongs are the most valued source of food in the northern coastal areas of Australia, both culturally and socially. As well as being an important source of protein, dugongs are a source of oil, which is highly prized for its medicinal qualities. Dugong hunting confers certain social status on the hunters; they are usually hunted for ceremonial and other special occasions within the community.

Dugongs are protected now, but Islanders continue to hunt them because the activity has a spiritual significance for them. Arguments rage because dugong numbers are decreasing, making them endangered, but Islanders claim they aren't hunting any more than they always have over the centuries, and archaeological evidence seems to back that up. If dugongs are getting rarer, it's maybe because their habitat is being destroyed for some other reason, such as global warming.

Turtle and dugong are both caught using whap spears, made from the wongai tree. Whaps have intricate carvings on them and are very heavy, with a club-like bit on the end. There are two types of point – three-pronged for catching turtles and one-pronged with barbs for dugong. Almost all dugongs are harpooned at sea, from a canoe in the past and a dinghy today, which requires great skill and patience. Hunters would get close up, then leap off and spear them.

Aboriginal and Torres Strait Islander groups have strong beliefs about the hunting, gathering and eating of foods. Different clans are assigned different totems and in some cases individuals are given personal totems when they are born. It is customary not to eat, kill or harm your totem, although in some tribes there are exceptions for special occasions, such as ceremonies. The diamond stingray (Yama) is the totem of the Wuthathi tribe of Shelbourne Bay, northern Queensland. The stingray is also the totem emblem for some Torres Strait Islanders. Sharks are a totem of the South Australian Ramindjeri people and they are forbidden to hunt them. This is also the case for the Murray Islanders, whose 19th-century carved stone shark reflects the long-term spiritual and cultural importance that sharks have had to the Islanders. There is a story about a Murray Island man and his son, who had an accident at sea and lost their boat. During the night as they waited to be rescued, sharks brushed past their legs. The Murray Islanders believe that the sharks did not attack the man and his son because the shark, their totem animal, protected them.

Stingray and shark are valued by other Islanders as a food and the livers, which contain good quantities of iron and vitamins, are given to babies and old people to make them strong. The boiled liver of a ray is said to be a cure for constipation. Otherwise the livers are mixed with the flesh, which is washed to improve its taste. Tiger, great white and bull sharks are all common, as well as less predatory sharks. Octopus are gathered on the early morning low tides, when the reefs surrounding the islands are dry, and only the lagoons have a little bit of water. When the sun starts to rise, the octopus return to holes in the seagrass beds and reef, where they cover themselves with coral. Otherwise, they can only be found in deeper, colder waters, and also at night when they can be speared from the reef in a low tide.

Left and above: *Modern power tools are now used to make whap spears. The tip is left thick to give weight and impetus to the harpoon when it is thrown. The shaft is smoothed with a piece of broken porcelain (in the past they used the tusk of a wild boar), then different clan designs are engraved on it. On the one above, designs representing an emu, snake and crocodile can be seen. Finally the spear point is inserted.*

Above: *Depressions in a rock caused when Islanders used it to sand down their war clubs.*

Around 32 species of sea snake have been recorded in Australian waters, and almost all are venomous. They are believed to have evolved from land snakes. Yellow-bellied and olive sea snakes are common in the warm waters of the Torres Strait. Sea snakes have specialised flattened tails for swimming and have valves over their nostrils, which are closed underwater. They differ from eels in that they don't have gill slits and they have scales. Because they need to breathe air, they are usually found in shallow water where they swim about the bottom feeding on fish, fish eggs and eels. They are aggressive only in the winter, during mating season, but they are curious and won't hesitate to 'taste' anything that looks like reasonable prey, or is deemed to be a potential predator.

Spines of stingrays and shark cartilage were used singly or in clusters to tip spears or arranged as a series of barbs; this made them valuable items to trade with inland peoples. Sharks' teeth made good drills and could be embedded in a wooden club or sword and shark skin made an excellent sandpaper.

The shells from crustaceans were widely used by the Islanders. Pearl shells in particular were used as decoration. Necklaces, nose decorations, pendants, belts, armbands, earrings and other items of symbolic importance were made from a variety of shells. Giant clams were used as implements for collecting rainwater and making axe heads, hoes and chisels. Baler shells were useful containers and cooking pots, and good for baling out canoes. Shells also functioned as spoons, scrapers, knives, cups and cooking vessels.

The islands were poor in material resources, particularly during monsoon season, so trade was developed between them and the New Guinea and Australian coast. The Eastern and Western Islands tended to trade with New Guinea while the southern Islands traded with the aboriginal people of Cape York. Islanders traded pearl shell, turtle shell, stone tools and human heads from their defeated enemies in return for domestic utensils, weapons, canoes, feathers and ochre. This trade was essential in maintaining life on many of the islands.

Above: *Crabs that have been cooked on a fire on the beach.*

Previous pages: *The view from Horn Island at sunset.*

Trade links were cemented through marriage and kinship ties. The Islanders' sailing skills and ocean-going canoes allowed them to extend their trading routes further afield. They tended to travel in small fleets so they had more protection from attack. They developed trade routes well into the north and south, and by the time the Europeans arrived, they were old hands at dealing with foreigners.

The traditional economic independence and reliance on island trade changed with the arrival of European settlers. Their discovery of pearls in the 1860s led to an influx of people from all over the region (Japanese, Malaysians, Filipinos, Micronesians and Europeans), especially to Thursday Island, which became the main settlement. By 1877, sixteen firms were established on Thursday Island, employing 700 people and using more than 100 pearl-luggers. European boat owners employed mostly Japanese divers, many of whom were indentured labourers, working for free in order to repay a debt, such as the cost of their passage to Australia.

The pearling industry was incredibly important to the Islanders, and has a long, at times dark, history. Before white explorers saw the benefits of this trade, local people had been collecting shells regularly, trading them with other islands and the continents to the north and south of the Strait. When white men arrived, the local people were encouraged to work without wages, diving naked into the waters with no oxygen or masks. The supply in coastal waters soon dried up, and they were forced to dive into deep, often dangerous waters, to find more shells.

According to John Singe, author of *Torres Strait: People and History*, the conditions of employment were dangerous and 'unspeakably squalid and dirty', causing untimely deaths and many accidents. In 1893, measures taken to regulate the industry and to prevent improper employment of aboriginals and Islanders were made by the Queensland parliament and wages were required to be paid in front of an inspector.

When rudimentary diving suits were invented, the industry was revolutionised. Divers could now go much deeper, stay underwater for longer periods, and collect more shells and pearls. We met up with a former diver, 'Seaman Dan', and saw first-hand the helmets they used to use, which were screwed onto canvas suits and fed oxygen from a tube on the surface. There were three glass 'windows' in the helmet, allowing divers to see out, but they were small and thickly lensed. The divers cleaned them with coffee grounds and vinegar to prevent them from misting up while underwater. They wore lead-weighted boots, which kept them down on the seabed while they frantically scooped oysters into a bag.

Seaman Dan is something of a local hero, and for good reason. He was born in 1929 on Thursday Island. His grandfather was a boat captain from Jamaica and his great-grandmother was a chief's daughter from Great New Caledonia. In the late 1940s and 1950s, he worked as a captain and pearl diver, gathering pearl and trochus shells in the Coral, Arafura and Timor Seas.

It was nice to hear stories of those days first-hand, from someone who had been through it, because the whole culture has gone now. Seaman Dan said divers were recruited at young ages, and usually paid low wages – or by the 'ton' of shell they collected. Pearls were rare and when they were found, the profits went mainly to the owners of the companies and luggers, with only a small percentage paid to the divers themselves. Waters were infested with sharks and other hostile marine creatures, and there was a serious risk of death from the 'bends', a condition that occurs when divers are brought up from the depths too quickly.

The bends, also known as 'decompression sickness', cause gas bubbles to form in a diver's body, causing itching skin, rashes, joint pain, sensory system failure, paralysis and death. To avoid this, divers must make period stops in their ascent from the sea's depths, and the number of these is dependent upon how deep they are submerged. The practice of making decompression stops is called 'staged decompression'. During the stop, the microbubbles present after every dive leave the diver's body safely through their lungs. If they are not given enough time to leave safely or more bubbles are created than can be eliminated naturally, the bubbles grow in size and number causing the symptoms and injuries of decompression sickness.

Seaman Dan recalled several occasions when this happened to him, during which he nearly lost his life and had to be rapidly resubmerged to prevent almost certain death. He also told me the story of one young diver whose helmet was not properly screwed on, causing water to rise in the chamber, which drowned him. Some 30 to 40 luggers were in the area at the time and all joined the search and rescue but the man's body was never found

Above: *The type of diving helmet that Seaman Dan used.*

Above right: *Now a well-known folk singer, Seaman Dan was lucky to survive his pearl diving days because the graveyards round here are full of the bodies of pearl divers.*

Page 259: *A painting on the side of a supermarket on Iam Island depicts the brutal past of the Islanders (which is never far from the present).*

as it had drifted off in the strong currents. Seaman Dan laughed as he told me about how sharks would circle as you waited at decompression stops and you would blow bubbles (which sharks don't like) to try and make them move on to the next man and leave you alone! Apart from the bends, and sharks, cyclones were a huge risk. Between 1908 and 1935, four cyclones hit the pearling fleet at sea; around 100 boats were destroyed and 300 men were killed.

Today, Dan is a well-known musician, with a repertoire that includes blues, hula, slow-jazz and pearling songs, which reflect the many cultures and traditions found in the Torres Strait and various other places he has lived, including Darwin and Broome in Australia, and Papua New Guinea. He remembers his pearling days with some fondness, but is clearly still amazed at the risks they took to find the pearls. Some sources claim that the mortality rate among pearl divers was 50 per cent.

Pearls obtained from the Torres Strait found a ready market in the clothing industry in the United States and England, especially for buttons and buckles.

The Torres Strait supplied over half the world demand for pearls in the 1890s, and pearl shell and 'mother of pearl' were used to make buttons, cutlery, hair combs, jewellery, furniture inlays and art objects. In the early 20th century, the government's 'White Australia Policy' restricted immigration to mostly white Europeans, creating a problem for the pearling industry, which was entirely reliant upon cheap, 'expendable' labour from Asia. As a solution to this, the government recruited twelve divers from the British Navy as pearl divers. Unfortunately, nearly all of them died, so an exception was made allowing the pearling town of Broome, which was the centre of the industry at this time, to continue recruiting Asians. In 1904, the London Missionary Society established a company to operate a trading station on Badu Island to sell the products of the Torres Strait Island fishing boats, and the pearling industry became central to the islands. During the First and Second World Wars, industry ceased when the Islanders enlisted (see page 273), and when Japanese divers were imprisoned in prisoner of war camps. Then, with the development of plastic, and a dwindling supply of ready workers after the war, the pearl shell industry declined, as merchants turned to farmed pearls instead of wild.

In the 17th, 18th and 19th centuries, the Torres Strait was known to seamen as the 'Terror Straits' and the islands were called 'Devil Islands', because many of the Islanders were fierce warriors, headhunters and, in some places, cannibals. Some of their art shows human skulls adorning posts, and we know that skulls were traded for other resources. The activities of these people have filtered down through the years in island legend, and also in the diaries and journals of travellers to the area. These stories aren't ancient history, but just under the surface as far as I'm concerned.

One such story is that of the *Charles Eaton*, a barque that sailed from Sydney harbour in 1834 carrying calico and lead. Twenty-five crewmen and six passengers were on board when the ship ran aground on the Detached Reef, in the Torres Strait. Five seamen escaped in the only boat that would float. The others built two large rafts and drifted off on it, hoping to be rescued.

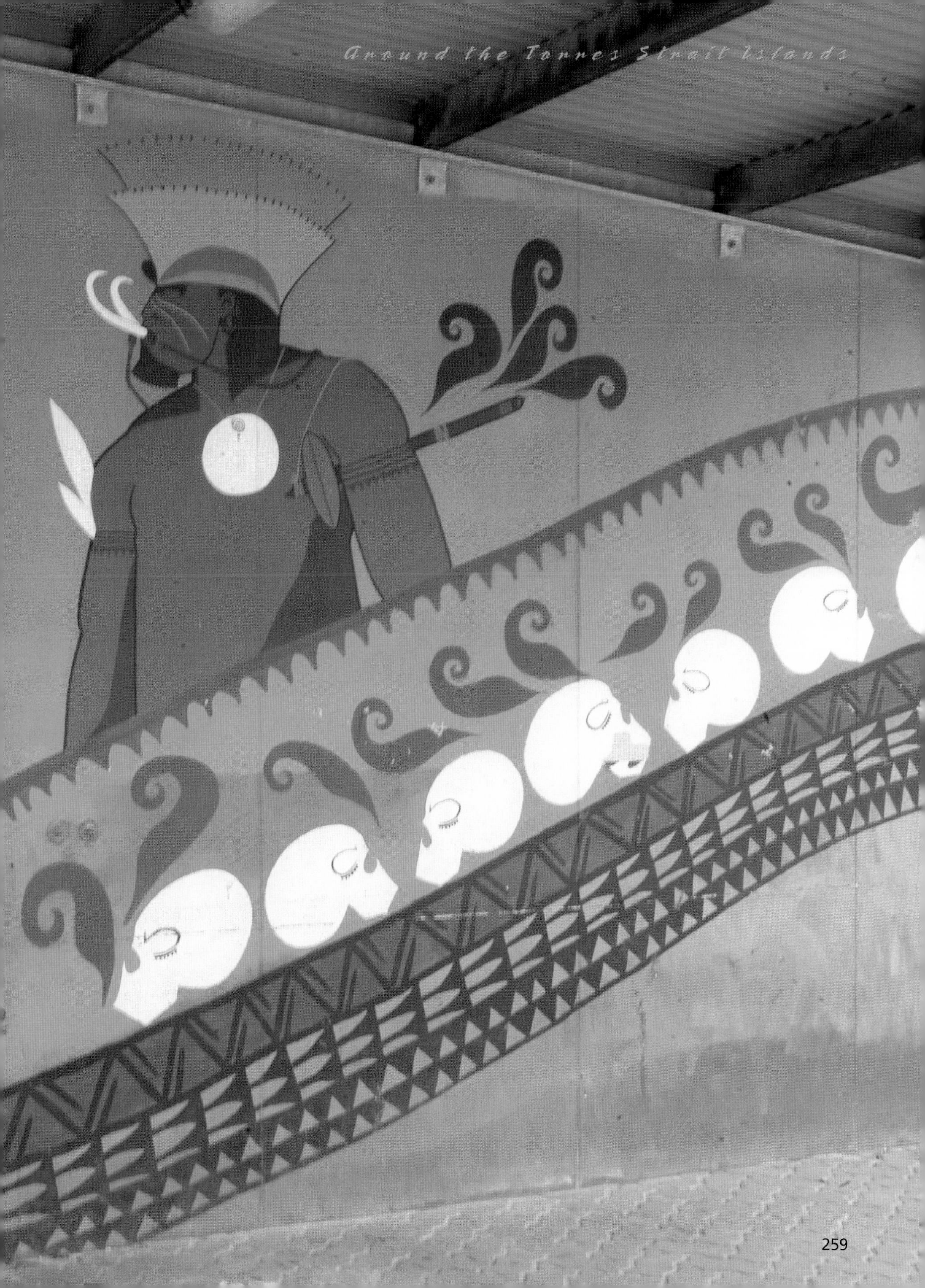

Three days later, some Islanders pulled up in a canoe beside one raft and invited the occupants on board. They were taken to an island called Boydan and instructed to walk to the other side to get water – but there they found there wasn't any. When they got back, they were all clubbed to death by the grinning natives – all except cabin boy John Ireland and William Sexton, both aged fourteen. They watched, petrified, as the victims' heads were lined up around a large fire.

The next day they were taken to another island, Pullan, where they met two children, George and William D'Oyley, from the other raft, and learned that all the adults on it had been beheaded as well. The boys were separated and legend has it that they were traded to Island families for a bunch of bananas each. Two of the boys were killed and eaten, while William D'Oyley and John Ireland were adopted by the native families.

It wasn't until an English convict ship, the *Mangles*, laid into port at Murray Island to trade with the Islanders, probably well over a year later, that John Ireland was discovered. John saw the ships and shouted out 'We're survivors of the *Charles Eaton*', his fair hair confirming the plausibility of his story. Although the ship sailed off without the two boys, the captain raised the alarm and another ship, the *Tigris,* returned later to rescue them. Their search for the other members of the ship's party and the two surviving boys was fruitless but on another island they found a heart and a human face made of turtle skulls, with 47 human skulls attached, including one of the boys' mothers. Her head had been bashed in but her hair was still trapped in it, allowing identification.

In 1869, a schooner called *Sperweer* under the helm of Captain Gascoigne was found on Prince of Wales Island with the remains of 28 people on board, all massacred and beheaded. A search party found their headless bodies in trees on the island, while the native Kaurareg people were wearing their clothes and jewellery and had made decorations out of parts of their revolvers.

There are countless stories of murders and massacres, sometimes in retribution for perceived slights against the Islanders (some stories tell of parties whose members attacked or raped the Islands' women), or sometimes out of fear or determination to protect their lands. In some of the islands, anyone shipwrecked was considered to have been rejected by the sea – a powerful and symbolic entity in native mythology – and therefore castaways received horrific treatment. Some had their eyeballs pulled out while still alive; their heads were chopped off, cooked and then eaten. The tongue was saved and wrapped in paperbark, then attached to the bows of their canoes as a charm. They said to the tongue, 'Call the turtles for me,' believing that in this way Islanders retain power over their victims.

A tiny uninhabited island called Booby Island was said to be the best place to aim for in the event of shipwreck in the Strait, because Islanders were afraid to go there. Mariners left dried food and water in a cave to help anyone who was cast ashore, and they also left letters in the cave that could be picked up by passing ships and taken on to their destination – a kind of unmanned post office.

These goings-on make the story of Barbara Thompson all the more amazing. Barbara was a young Scotswoman (maiden name Crawford), who migrated with her parents from Aberdeen in Scotland to Sydney when she was eight. Her father was a tinsmith, although he later turned his hand to other jobs, and eventually spent a period in prison for handling stolen goods. When she was sixteen, Barbara eloped with a seaman named William Thompson, and they were married at Moreton Bay, a large bay on the eastern coast of Australia, about 19 kilometres from Brisbane. The newlyweds joined the crew of a cutter, known as the *America*, and with an old sailor and two additional crew members, set out to salvage whale oil from a wreck in the Torres Strait in 1844. Interestingly, Thompson had been asked by the explorer Leichhardt to accompany him on his journey to Port Essington (see pages 35-36), but he decided instead to head for the bounty of the seas.

The trip was fraught with disaster, and it was difficult to find the wreck. Two of the crewmen were drowned when a dingy that had been overfilled with firewood sank, and the sailors ran out of provisions, living instead on fish and other marine life. Just north of Cape York, in December 1844, the ship was hit by a sudden squall and driven onto a reef off Horn Island. Barbara clung to the wreckage, while the remaining crew struggled to reach the shore, but they all drowned in the process. Barbara was rescued by some natives in a canoe and taken to Prince of Wales Island, where she was greeted by one of the leaders,

known as 'Peaqui'. He thought she was a reincarnation of his daughter Giom, who had tragically died at sea, so she was given Giom's name and allowed to live with them. Imagine her shock and distress: she had watched her husband drown, been rescued by peoples said to be cannibals, and now they were talking away to her in a language she couldn't understand.

Barbara was claimed into the native social structure, and treated with great respect and kindness. She found it hard to learn the ways of the Kaurareg people and was soon demoted to looking after children in the camp. She would sing folk songs to help her remember her native tongue and would often cry as she looked at the wedding ring that she had hung around her neck in a handkerchief. Eventually the Islanders threw the ring and all of her other possessions into the fire, believing them to be the source of her unhappiness. This must have been a huge blow to the young Scotswoman, as her last links to her past were taken from her.

For the next five years she was concealed and protected, learning the language and the ways of this tribe. When ships came past the Kaurareg painted her black and when a barbaric white man on a neighbouring island expressed his wish to marry her, they hid her deep down Hammond Creek (it was thought that this man, who went by the name of Weenie, was in fact an escaped convict from down south, although it was later discovered that he was probably a Dutch seaman who had been cast adrift). Despite the many kindnesses of the Islanders, Barbara suffered immensely while in their care. She damaged her knee, causing her to limp heavily, and she got horrific burns up one side of her body after her Pandanus mat caught fire while she slept. Recurring infections caused her to become blind in one eye.

There are two fascinating first-hand accounts of her eventual rescue, both by men aboard the HMS *Rattlesnake*, on which she eventually escaped. John MacGillivray was the ship zoologist, who published his account in his 1852 book, *Narrative Of The Voyage Of H.M.S. Rattlesnake*. While on board the *Rattlesnake*, Barbara dictated her memories of her time with the Islanders to Englishman Oswald Walters Brierly, who had studied marine matters and art, and came to Australia in 1842. For five years he managed Benjamin Boyd's whaling activities on the southern coast of New South Wales before he was invited to join Captain Owen Stanley on the *Rattlesnake* as an artist in 1848. It

Above: *The beach on Prince of Wales Island where Barbara Thompson was held prisoner for five years.*

Pages 263-264: *Booby Island was a sanctuary for anyone shipwrecked in the Torres Strait because Islanders refused to come here. Ships left salt beef and flasks of fresh water in a cave, and all you had to do next was get across around 1,600 kilometres to Timor or Moreton Bay to reach safety.*

was in his subsequent journals and accounts that he told the story of Barbara Thompson in full.

During the five years that Barbara was in the Torres Strait Islands, she watched dozens of ships travel through the area without anchoring near her island. The Islanders kept a close eye on her, and did not allow her to trade or to set foot on Cape York, where most of the ships laid to anchor. Her fellow tribesmen traded regularly with the whites, and had visited the *Rattlesnake* a year earlier at Cape York. When Barbara showed interest in their dealings, they became suspicious and, as MacGillivray says, 'watched her more narrowly than before'.

On their second visit, a year later, the HMS *Rattlesnake* again docked at Cape York, and Barbara successfully persuaded some of the Islanders that she should be brought to the mainland within a short distance of where the ships lay. The islanders believed she didn't intend to leave them because she had been with them so long, and had been so well treated, and they allowed her to go when she said that 'she felt a strong desire to see the white people once more and shake hands with them; adding that she would be certain to procure some axes, knives, tobacco, and other much prized articles.'

They took her to a small island, just a stone's throw from where the ships were anchored in Evans Bay, yet she was unable to cross to them for fear of what the Islanders might do to her if she escaped. The truth is that she would probably have been killed. After two days, when some of the Islanders were boarding a canoe to cross to the mainland, she jumped aboard at the last minute, probably helped by one of her close friends, Tomagugu, and was allowed to travel with them.

They landed at a sandy bay on the western side of Cape York, and she stumbled across to Evans Bay, hampered by her leg injury, and limping heavily. She was naked apart from a few leaves, and deeply tanned and blistered by the sun. Only her fair hair made it possible for the sailors to believe that she was not a native, but even so several members of the *Rattlesnake* (including Brierly) who were out shooting walked past her, thinking her a 'gin'.

MacGillivray says that a small party of island men followed to detain her, but arrived too late. Three were brought on board with her, at her request, and they were each given an axe and other presents to thank them for saving her.

Barbara was reluctant to admit that she wanted to leave the Islands, particularly in front of the Islanders who had treated her with such kindness, and became agitated. Her English was poor, and she struggled to find words to make her wishes known, alternating English with Kaurareg language.

Right: *The tiny island (above right) where Barbara Thompson spent her last two days as a prisoner, just a stone's throw away from Evans Bay (right) where the Rattlesnake was moored. It must have been unbearably frustrating for her to watch the English sailors on the beach but be unable to get across to them.*

Finally, she said: 'Sir, I am a Christian, and would rather go back to my own friends.'

Once on board the *Rattlesnake*, Brierly confirms that she was *'received … with the greatest kindness and a cabin being prepared for her, she was amply supplied with material for clothing and every comfort, and her health and general appearance began to improve rapidly. Though without education she had been remarkably observing and as she recovered fully the use of her own language, gave the most interesting accounts of the customs of the native. She said that she had tried to keep up the recollection of her own language by singing what songs she knew when she lay down at night. She spoke well of her treatment by the natives, and said that when she was wrecked, they did not attempt to take away her clothes, which she wore afterwards for a long time …'*

Barbara began to tell the crew of the *Rattlesnake* everything she had experienced in her five years on the islands. The natives were incredibly fond of her, and apparently visited her regularly on the ship. One man in particular, Boroto, was extremely reluctant to let her go, and made scenes on board in order to have her released into his care. No one was sure why he was so adamant that she returned, but island legend relates that Barbara gave birth to two children during her stay and it is likely that Boroto was the father. MacGillivray says that Boroto tried regularly to convince her to go back to live with him, and eventually left the ship in a fury, threatening that if she was ever caught on shore again, they would remove her head and take it back with them to Muralug. Not surprisingly, she never again ventured on shore at Cape York.

During her time aboard the *Rattlesnake*, Barbara provided an incredibly illuminating account of her life

Top left: *The isthmus Barbara walked across towards Evans Bay and freedom at last.*

Left: *This may be the remains of a well the Rattlesnake sailors dug at the back of the beach in which to wash their clothes.*

with the Islanders, dictating her memories to Oswald Brierly, and providing a wealth of insight into the people, their culture, history, practices, and daily life. To this day, we know more about the early Torres Strait Islanders from Barbara's recollections than from any other source. Her information would subsequently allow many white men to create and maintain good relations with the Islanders, because they were able to understand the language to some degree, and to respect their beliefs and practices.

Barbara told Brierly that she was not married, and that Boroto and two other men, Alikia and Tomagugu, were like brothers to her, having been the first to find her when her ship was wrecked almost five years earlier. It was Tomagugu, a sensible man who liked and admired Barbara, who had been instrumental in allowing her to travel to the mainland to trade with the whites, and he subsequently facilitated her escape.

She said clearly to MacGillivray that 'on only one occasion was any improper liberty attempted by the men – she was fortunately saved by a friend who soundly thrashed the intending ravisher, an old man well known to us'. In several places in her recollection, she denies having had a husband or children, and, in fact, says she objected to the practice of being left behind with the other wives to prepare food while the men went out to trade with incoming vessels. However, I think it's probable that she declined to mention her children for fear of being left behind by the *Rattlesnake*. One of the elders we met told us that inter-island adoption was quite a common practice and that Barbara's brown babies were adopted and cared for after her escape. Island adoption still happens; while we were there, we met a woman who had had a child for an infertile woman on another island. It's not legal but it still happens.

About six months later, Barbara returned to her parents in Sydney, where she eventually married and had a family. Although her account, transcribed by Brierly, is unbelievably complete, and most facts have subsequently been verified, it's still hard to imagine what the experience was like for her psychologically. I can only think she must have been a remarkably strong woman – another gritty Scot, like John McDouall Stuart. The Islanders tell her heart-rending story with pride, and to this day show great fondness for the white woman who lived among them for so many years.

On Saturday 1 July 1871, some visitors arrived in the Torres Strait who would change island life forever. The Reverends Samuel MacFarlane and A.W. Murray of the London Missionary Society anchored at Darnley Island, along with eight Polynesian mission teachers and their wives. They must have been nervous, given the well-known fierce reputation of the Islanders, but they came on shore and began spreading their message of Christianity. One by one, island elders were converted and allowed the reverends to set up mission stations on each island to further spread the word and schools to educate the children. The first substantial church-type building was constructed in 1881, and it was replaced by Holy Trinity Church (1919–38).

Known as 'the Coming of the Light', the arrival of the missionaries changed many aspects of island life and is celebrated each year by festivities throughout the islands, including a kup mari feast. The kup mari is a ground oven built in a shallow pit lined with stones. When the stones are white hot, the food is put on top of them and the oven is sealed by placing more stones, leaves and wet sacks on top. The kup mari can cook a whole pig, or a turtle in its shell, keeping in all the juices.

Torres Straits Islanders are now predominantly practising Christians, but they blend the teachings of the church with their traditional culture and beliefs. While we were on Yam Island, we went to a place where war clubs are made and our guide suddenly went very quiet. I looked around and noticed an old coconut shell, blackened with age, on which a human face had been carved. I discovered that this is used in male initiation ceremonies that still go on here. They have to drink from the coconut and if they spill a drop it means they are going to die.

Throughout our travels on the Islands, I was aware of this mixture of modern lifestyles – televisions, fridges, proper houses – and some attitudes that still hark back to the time when it was known as the Terror Strait.

If the conversion of the Islanders came as a surprise to those who believed them to be dangerous maneaters, the Second World War brought the Torres Strait Islanders into great repute, when their dignity and warrior spirit was instrumental in defending Australia from the Japanese invasions.

Above: *A coconut shell carved into a human face, evidence of the continuation of traditional ceremonies on the Islands. This was handed round for boys to drink from at initiation ceremonies and it was said that if they spilled a drop, they would die.*

A few years before the invasion of Pearl Harbour, the Australian government had begun to suspect that there would be a war in the Pacific. In 1940, they decided that they would need defences in the north, with advanced operational air bases. Horn Island was chosen, not only because it was big and flat, with good space for a landing strip and a wharf, but also because it was strategically vital, right in the centre of the Islands. The Australians knew that if they could hold Horn Island, the Japanese would be unlikely to take the Strait. Without the Strait, they would be unable to bomb far south into the Australian mainland because there would be nowhere for them to refuel. For this reason, Horn Island became a stronghold during the Second World War.

On 14 March 1942, the Japanese first raided the area, and throughout the war they would drop some 500 bombs over the Islands. Interestingly, only a few islands were hit and none were raided; some may have been left untouched because the graves of Japanese pearl divers were located there. In the early months of the war, Islanders were not permitted to join the army, navy or airforce but in 1940, the government changed its mind. Of this limited population, an unbelievable 880 men enlisted, leaving only about ten men of enlistment age behind to care for the women and children, and to hunt. This represented a huge commitment to the Australian people on the part of the Islanders, particularly in view of the fact that they didn't have full rights as Australian citizens. They weren't allowed to vote, and they received only a third of the pay that non-native soldiers received. And yet they signed up in their droves, and lent their fighting spirit to the cause, taking great pride in their contribution.

The Islands became a crucial operating centre during the war, and more than 8,000 men served here, with 5,000 stationed, including Americans and Australians. The Torres Strait Light Infantry of about 2,000 men was a unique battalion in that almost all of its enlisted men were Torres Strait Islanders, making it the only indigenous Australian battalion. Throughout the war the battalion was based on Horn Island and Thursday Island, where it formed an integral part of the Islands' defences.

Other Islanders headed south, where they joined other battalions and gained respect and admiration for their skill and attitude. The interaction between the indigenous populations and the white members of the armed forces was to prove hugely valuable. They formed strong bonds, and shared a wealth of information. The Islanders taught the mainlanders how to fish and collect seafood to supplement a poor and tasteless army diet. They eventually formed the 'marine supply platoon', which provided fish and other seafood to hospital patients and serving members of the forces. It was also a great experience for the Torres Strait Islanders, who before this time had been very much a community of separate islands with varying practices, who regularly fought with and raided one another. The war united them against an external common enemy, to defend their lands.

Their contribution to the war was supremely important, and their warriorlike spirit was much commented upon and commended. One key general called them 'wonderful soldiers, as good as those in the British army'.

Horn Island was the second most attacked target in Australia (only Darwin was hit more), and some 182 bombs landed on the island and surrounding waters. Submarines patrolled the Strait and sea mines were laid by both the Japanese and the Americans, which would prove hugely dangerous during the war and in its aftermath. In all, 181 men lost their lives in the Torres Strait, including 82 civilians who died when their boat was targeted by a Japanese submarine.

Yam Island was also heavily bombed. The reason for this is unclear, but it is believed that the Japanese became frustrated after the loss of three planes at the hands of the Americans, and came looking for them. The airmen had been taken to Darwin, so the Japanese machine-gunned a merchant vessel, injuring thirteen, and launched a sustained attack on villages on Yam Island for no obvious reason.

This was a hugely difficult time for the women and children of the Torres Straits, who had no men to protect them or to hunt for food. They moved inland, into caves and mangrove swamps when their villages came under attack, setting up bush camps where they survived for between four and five years. They grew gardens, containing yams, cassava, bananas and other

Above: *Three families took refuge in this cave during World War II. It was a cramped space but provided them with much-needed sanctuary.*

produce, and they were able to catch shellfish and do a little trapping, but staple parts of their diet, such as dugong, were missing.

These were hard times for the Islanders. The seas were impossible to negotiate because of the landmines and submarines, and they had little if any contact with their men. Until coast watches were set up to look for aircraft, submarines and other threats to the islands, when two men came with radios, they had no news of their menfolk and surely feared the worst. I met some women, Lavi and Salu, who were just young girls when a Japanese Zero warplane began strafing the beach with bullets and they had to run for shelter in nearby caves – but only thirteen non-combatant Islanders were killed during the war.

It took many years after the war for the status quo to return in the islands. Many men found it difficult to come back to native life after their spell in the army and the pearl industry, previously a big employer, had ground to a halt,

Above: *Lavi and Salu sitting on the beach where they lived as children. They remembered being terrified when a submarine surfaced just offshore.*

Pages 278-9: *Ilana cooking mud mussels over a fire.*

so many Islanders moved to the mainland where they took up more Westernised lifestyles. They were changed people. They had great pride in their achievements, and a strong appreciation of themselves as citizens, which eventually led them to demand rights as citizens of Australia. It took a further almost 20 years before they were given the right to vote, but their experiences in the army helped to strengthen their resolve to fight for equality.

Islanders had become frustrated during the war about the fact that they received only a percentage of the pay given to white soldiers and because of this, and several other matters that had been causing frustration, the 'A', 'B' and 'C' companies of the battalion had gone on strike in December 1943. In February 1944, the army agreed to increase their pay to two-thirds of that of the white soldiers, but it took until 1980 for the soldiers to receive full back-pay for their war service.

The Torres Strait Light Infantry Battalion was disbanded in 1946. 'C' Company was established in the Torres Strait in 1987 as a Regional Force Surveillance Unit (RFSU) responsible for sovereignty patrols in the Torres Strait. Many of the soldiers who serve in it today had fathers and grandfathers who fought in the Second World War.

Having long discarded their 'headhunter' and 'devil' reputations, Islanders now have a strong and united series of impressive, proud cultures that is overseen by the Torres Strait Regional Authority. Through their art and storytelling, they maintain some of their old belief systems and mythology, passing on information about their ancient practices and extraordinary history. And even today, they use age-old ceremonies to celebrate their culture, and to feast on the bountiful marine life surrounding their islands.

During my walkabout, I crossed the country, seeing sights I found both enchanting and awe-inspiring, and admiring the dignity of the native peoples, their art, their beliefs, and their staunch defence of their heritage. Stories are told, retold, and sung in the Australian continent and her islands, creating an incredible juxtaposition of new and old, and creating a magical tapestry of interwoven cultural threads. I was educated, fascinated and inspired by what I saw. If a walkabout is designed to clear the head and bring us back to nature and all that is important, my journeys had succeeded. There can be no doubt that I'll being going walkabout again.

Acknowledgements

The author would like to thank Gill Paul for all her amazing hard work and professionalism in making the book come together.

Thanks to the BBC crew:

Camera:	Barrie Foster
	Alan Duxbury (Alan's first trip with us since a helicopter crash in summer 2004 - welcome back!)
Sound:	Tim Green
	Andy Morton

Production:

Series Producer	Ben Southwell
Director	John Miller
Production Team:	Jo Fletcher
	Joe Hill
	Cassy Walkling

Thanks also to the following for their contribution to the programmes:

Les Hiddins, Syd Kyle-Little, JuJu Wilson, Pat Lowe, the aboriginal people of the Kimberleys, Barry Ralph, Rick Moore, Colin Harris, Reg Dodd, Seaman Dan, Vanessa Seekee and Enid Tom.

Photographs

The pictures come from the photographic archives of Ray Mears, with some extras by Joe Hill, and were mostly taken specifically for this book. The Syd Kyle-Little photographs are used by his kind permission.

Additional photos have been supplied by: National Portrait Gallery (page 17); National Library of Australia (pages 28, top, and 29, both pictures); Mary Evans Picture Library (page 28, bottom).

Every reasonable effort has been made to contact the copyright holders, but if there are any errors or omissions, Hodder & Stoughton will be pleased to insert the appropriate acknowledgement in any subsequent printing of this publication.